The Grammatically Correct Handbook

The Grammatically Correct Handbook

The Correct Handbook

ELLIE GROSSMAN

A Lively **and**
Unorthodox
Review **of**
Common
English,
for the
Linguistically
Challenged

HYPERION
New York

Library of Congress Cataloging-in-Publication Data

Grossman, Ellie.
The grammatically correct handbook : a lively and unorthodox
review of common English, for the
linguistically challenged / Ellie Grossman.
p. cm.
Includes index.
ISBN 0-7868-8169-0
1. English language—Grammar—Handbooks,
manuals, etc. I. Title.
PE1112.G69 1997
428.2—DC20   96–42460
CIP

Book design by Richard Oriolo

FIRST EDITION

10 9 8 7 6 5 4 3 2 1

For—alphabetically—
Matthew Faber
and Samantha Faber,
with love

Contents

❸ Miscellaneous Misunderstandings (Hmm . . .)   171

Acknowledgments

My thanks to:

Laurie Abkemeier

Bob Cochnar

Bill Longgood

Henry Morrison

Harvey Orkin

Rose Oosting

Sandra Pierson Prior

The Grammatically Correct Handbook

Introduction

What's wrong with the following? "The senator said that, just between him and me, his page had some pair of knockers."

"One in ten lawyers is lying when his lips are moving."

"Look at it this way: Fewer calories, less flab."

Absolutely nothing (barring slurs and sexism). Not that you'd know, considering the English you see and hear these days—and not just on *Geraldo*, either:

From a public relations agency mailing: "We look forward to seeing you at our infectious diseases dinner."

From a Pulitzer Prize–winning reporter, on National Public Radio: "[The story] was initially broke by a reporter. . . ."

From Jim Lehrer on, well, you know Jim Lehrer: "To whom did she give this money to?" (Jimmy! Jim-bo!)

That's not to say *I* don't make mistakes every now and then. In conversation, I catch myself saying "than me," and using "they" to refer to "someone." ("Hey, everybody spills things," said Michael Moore, commiserating with Exxon.) But, generally, I don't make mistakes (in English, you understand). I'm old enough to know better. I was taught English by Miss Thomas, Mrs. Pringle, Mrs. Marmur, et al., in the days when English teachers knew what they were talking about. Good grammar, correct usage, and proper pronunciation all became part of me.

Mind you, my teachers followed the time-honored maxim, "God forbid we should teach English in English," which means they wallowed in their own particular jargon—"subjunctive," "nominative," "accusative," "future perfect," etc.—which is precisely the trouble with most books on English usage and grammar. They get hung up on fancy words and definitions, instead of just telling you what to do. Straight out.

Why shouldn't students, job seekers, job holders, and language lovers be able to correct the current, most common English boners, quickly and painlessly (and be entertained in the bargain)?

No complicated rules.

No dense explanations.

No jargon. (If you didn't understand "intransitive" back then, why should you have to try now?)

Now, with the help of this book, it's possible. And once you know what you're talking about, you can impress Mom, win that scholarship, nail down that job, get that raise, and, yes, conquer the guy/gal of your dreams! All in good English.

THE GRAMMATICALLY
CORRECT HANDBOOK
THE GRAMMATICALLY
CORRECT HANDBOOK
THE GRAMMATICALLY
CORRECT HANDBOOK
THE GRAMMATICALLY
CORRECT HANDBOOK
THE GRAMMATICALLY
CORRECT HANDBOOK
THE GRAMMATICALLY
CORRECT HANDBOOK
THE GRAMMATICALLY
CORRECT HANDBOOK
THE GRAMMATICALLY

1 Mistaken Identities

(Oops!)

As **Y**ou

Like **I**t?

Or **N**ot

Like me, are you creative? Why not try origami, the ancient Japanese art of paper folding? All you need are some paper and your two hands. With a little practice, in no time at all, you'll be amazing your friends with your paper creations!

Come with me now, as we cruise *like explorers* through the wonderful world of fascinating folds.

We'll begin with a miniature Boeing 767.

STEP 1: Take a sheet of paper that looks *like a rectangle*.

STEP 2: Fold corner A crosswise to corner C. Pull corner D below corner B to a depth of 3/8 inch. Crease. Smooth.

STEP 3: Tuck edge E into the resulting pocket. As you do, make a peak fold along edge F, which will act *like a wing*.

STEP 4: Repeat Step 3 beginning with edge G. Refold. Press. Holding the figure with both hands, take folded edge H to the rolled fold. Press. Pull. Primp. Pray *like the devil*.

"Like" indicates that something (or someone) is *similar to* something (or someone) else:

> ➤ On Fridays, he dressed *like* George Washington.
> ➤ Sam Dunk looks *like* a koala bear.
> ➤ *Like* his other fans, Naomi would have died for a shock of Telly Savalas's hair.

"As," on the other hand, works like this:

> ➤ Nobody can do the fandango *as Blaise does.*
> ➤ "*As I've told you*, Fetlock, the honey locust tree does not produce honey or locusts!"
> ➤ *As indicated in the report*, Mr. Heath's gallbladder needs tuning.
> ➤ *As rumored*, the cow really did take up with the spoon, to the bull's amazement.

"As," you see, is often part of a *clause*, which consists of a *noun* and a *verb*. A clause is not a full sentence. "As" may also be part of a *phrase*. (But I promised not to use any jargon. Forget what I just said.)

As is also handy for comparisons, as in:

> ➤ The new begonias weren't *as waxy as* the old ones.
> ➤ Samara was
> *as* original *as* a fax
> *as* endearing *as* a thumb in your eye
> *as* much fun *as* being snowed in at the airport for seven hours with a gregarious mime—"For the last time, Mr. Bippy, shut up!"

POINTED TIP: Don't use "like" to mean "as if" or "as though." You must use "as."

➤ Rip Van Winkle yawned *as if* he'd been asleep for years.

➤ It's not *as though* this matters, but the squid has the largest eyes of any creature on earth, including Big Brother.

Quick Quiz

Circle the correct choice(s) in each of the following:

1. Mr. Bledsoe ran (like/as) the dickens when the process server showed up.
2. Natalie tossed her head. "I hate those natural cosmetics stores. All the products smell (like/as) the same rotten melon."
3. Ezra always balances his checkbook zestfully, (like/as) a pig in a cornfield.
4. "Just (like/as) I thought," cried Eric the Red, pointing to Greenland, "we've reached São Paulo!"
5. "Don't rub the lamp (like/as) a wimp," hollered the genie. "Rub it (like/as if) you mean it, or I'll never get the hell out of here!"
6. Friday acted (like/as) a friend to Robinson Crusoe, (like/as) any other smart castaway would; after all, Crusoe could cook up one scrumptious bouillabaisse.
7. "Just because it looks (like/as) a lily and smells (like/as) a lily, doesn't mean it's not a leek," said Bartholomew, (like/as if) he had just thought that up.
8. "(Like/As) I mentioned previously," said Mme Maya, "you'll be required to write a five-act play, just (like/as) Shakespeare did all these many years ago." Then she burped.
9. "She acts (like/as though) she were a kid," murmured Rollo, watching Aunt Lucina chew a tin can.

10. The Countess of Albacore spoke (like/as) a moron, but that didn't matter. It wasn't (like/as if) the count paid any attention, especially when the maid, Aphrodite, was in the room.

Answers

❶ **like** (Mr. Bledsoe believed in putting off forever, whatever he could get away with.)

❷ **like** (Those of you who disagree, raise your gritty oatmeal loofahs.)

❸ **like** (Ezra also tears painstakingly along perforated edges.)

❹ **as** (You're right. Eric didn't say that at all. Actually, he said, "If I hear, 'Are we there yet?' one more time from you guys . . . !")

❺ **like, as if** (Sure, Aladdin got his wishes, but like certain network stars, the genie was no picnic to work with.)

❻ **like, as** (Crusoe cooked so well, in fact, that Friday never told him there was a flourishing seaport just the other side of the croquet lawn.)

❼ **like, like, as if** (Bartholomew had some head on his shoulders.)

❽ **as, as** (Mme Maya taught creative writing three afternoons a week at the library, which was across from a discount liquor store.)

❾ **as though** (Baaaaaa.)

❿ **like, as if** (Don't feel bad for the countess. The butler, who resembled Phil Sims, was teaching her how to catch passes.)

BOTTOM LINE: *As* you pedal along *like* a hellcat on wheels, show the cop who stops you that you know how he (or she) feels. "I may look *like* a menace, but, *as* my mom will attest, I'm caring and dependable— so put away that ticket, Officer, and let's . . . hey, you listening to me, or what?"

Emigrate/

Immigrate

"Immigrate" does not mean *both* leaving one country *and* going to live in another. If it did, you wouldn't need "emigrate."

You "emigrate *from*" Nepal, and "immigrate *to*" Zimbabwe, which involves a whole new wardrobe.

Martha *emigrated from* Montpelier, Vermont, in the spring of 1978. The family felt it would be in her best interest if she started a new life somewhere else, so she left.

In those days, no one spoke out loud about a nervous breakdown. Just like today, there was a good deal of shame attached to having your marbles spill all over the floor, careering off furniture and tripping people up.

Fortunately, Martha had seen a TV special about Behemoth Island and decided to *immigrate to* its capital, Big Foot. The sun, the air, the soft grass were all to her liking and, after just a week, she wrote an ecstatic letter home:

Dear Mom and Dad,
Things couldn't be better. I'm so glad I left Vermont, although the idea of *emigrating* didn't sit well with me at first, as you know. Big Foot is lovely. The people are darling. Even though I'm an *immigrant* and unfamiliar with their customs, they treat me like a member of the family. I think I can live without "incident" here.
Love, Muffy.
P.S. Let me know when you run out of mango juice.

POINTED TIP: Emigrate starts with an "e," which stands for "out"; immigrate starts with "im," which is close to "in," which stands for "in."

In conclusion, you "emigrate" from the country you're leaving.

You "immigrate" to the country you're moving to, where life will be peaches and cream for, oh, six weeks.

That's how long it took before Muffy experienced a disconcerting "incident."

There she was, sitting on the lanai, enjoying a pint of vanilla yogurt, when out of the blue a spider *this big* crawled over her sandal and sent her shrieking off in the direction of the American embassy.

Muffy, unfortunately, had made a trip to the john during that TV special and had missed the part where the announcer said, "Big Foot is also home to spiders the size of an eggplant."

Was she always to be haunted by these horrid curds-and-whey-and-creepy-crawly episodes? (Yes)

Was there to be no peace in her future? (No)

Bummer.

BOTTOM LINE: It's impossible to "immigrate to" Country B, until you "emigrate from" Country A.

When His Prostate Went Bad, They Found Him Prostrate

"Let's see, now. Thank you for filling out our application, Mr. . . . Churchill, is it?"

"Yeah. That's the moniker. Choichill."

"How long have you lived here, Mr. Churchill?"

"I dunno. A munt, maybe."

"A 'munt'?"

"Give or take."

The co-op's managing agent put his pen to his lips. "I see, and how long did you live in, let's see . . . is that Fresno?"

"Nah. Frisco." Mr. Churchill crossed his legs and fixed his eyes on the managing agent. "What's the difference? I'm heah, now, ain't I?"

"Heh, heh," said the managing agent, striving to be sociable. "Well, perhaps you can tell me why you left San Francisco?" He attempted a smile, but his lips stuck to his teeth.

"My *prostrate* went bad and I needed a operation."

"You don't mean that," began the managing agent.

Mr. Churchill uncrossed his legs. "You callin' me a liar?"

The managing agent wiped his forehead. "No, no, no, of course not. 'Pros*tate*' is a male gland; 'pros*trate*' is when you're lying facedown on the floor, or totally exhausted."

"Facedown," Mr. Churchill repeated, savoring the word. "Yeah, I like that. Facedown. On the floor. Lots of my customers end up 'pros*trate*'!" He gave a low, rumbling laugh, and the managing agent joined him, an octave higher and just this side of hysteria.

"So," Mr. Churchill said, "when am I movin' in?"

The managing agent cleared his throat and chirped, "Tuesday?"

BOTTOM LINE: "Prostate" is the gland that often makes things difficult for men over fifty; **"prostrate"** can mean either lying facedown or absolutely, totally worn-out.

Oral/
Verbal

David and Goliath had an *oral* agreement to work out their differences through a "knock the gourd off Livia's head" competition. That's why David had only a slingshot on him that day. But when Goliath showed up, David took one look at him and said, "You've been carbo loading!" Goliath took a menacing step forward, poked David in the chest, and jeered, "Liar, liar, pants on fire!" Well, David had no choice but to get him to see things from a different position. But if they'd put things in writing to begin with Goliath would still be walking around today.

Usually, you hear "verbal" used incorrectly. The speaker really means "oral." "Oral" concerns something that has to do with the mouth, such as flossing or rinsing. It also means "spoken," not written, as in oral exams.

When you have a "verbal" agreement, you have an agreement via "words," as opposed to an understanding by means of Tibetan sand painting or hieroglyphics.

POINTED TIP: If your landlord agrees on the phone to let you stay beyond your lease, get him to sign a note to that effect. Don't go by an *oral* agreement, unless you *want* to end up moving back in with Marconi and his overwhelming collection of *Star Wars* memorabilia.

BOTTOM LINE: "Oral" means spoken, as in Twyla's endless "oral history" of her ins and outs in the storm door business. "Verbal" means "having to do with words," as in "Webster's verbal obsession was very annoying, irksome, and vexing to everyone but Roget."

Prone/
Supine

Ladies and gentlemen, boys and girls, welcome to the Flip-Top Circus!

We are delighted to present The Flying Contradictions! Acclaimed for their courage and timing, these spectacular trapeze artists have performed in every major capital of the world!

Proudly we direct your attention to the center ring—and The Flying Contradictions!

(drum roll)

"Well"—Josephina's aged fingers fluttered in her lap—"Mauritzio was miffed because I had accepted Mikhail's invitation for the weekend. I knew that, but I never expected him to pull his hands back after I flew somersaulting across the ring to his swing."

The reporter assumed an expression of shock. "What happened?"

"I fell. What was worse, I fell like a klutz, landing facedown. Prone."

Welling up, the reporter managed, "Were you hurt?"

"Well, I did catch my nose in the safety net, chafing a nostril—and there *was* the psychological damage." Josephina shuddered. "For years, I was unable to shake hands."

The reporter shaded his eyes.

"If I had not been so surprised," Josephina went on, "I would at least have landed gracefully, on my back. Supine." She took a breath. "Still," she went on, "it all turned out for the best."

".How so?"

"There was a young personal-injury lawyer in the audience. After the show, he came back and offered to represent me in a suit against Mauritzio, the management, the net makers . . ."

"Is that how you were able to buy this estate?" The reporter made a broad gesture.

"*And* the island it sits on, honey!"

Pretending to turn off his tape recorder, the reporter smiled. "Tell me, Ms. Buongusto, how did the incident affect your love life?"

You never know when "prone" or "supine" will come up in life as we know it, so it pays to know the difference: *prone*—facedown, on your stomach; *supine*—face up, on your back.

> **POINTED TIP:** If you take the U out of
>   S (U) P I N E ,
> that leaves SPINE! as in flat on your . . .

> **BOTTOM LINE:** When you're *prone*, you can do the breaststroke; when you're *supine*, you can do the backstroke; when the team you bet your Boy George lip print on loses the game, you may just *have* a stroke.

Bemused/

Amused

?
    ?
?   E
    ?   B   M

    ?   U

    ?   S

    ?   E

    ?   D

Captain Jirk took the bridge. "Take us into Pluto's orbit, Ensign
Flusher."

"Aye, aye, sir." Ensign Flusher depressed a score of indicators on his control panel, but nothing happened. "Captain, the ship seems to be locked in a magnogravity field. It won't respond to my commands."

Captain Jirk frowned. "Mr. Crock," he said, "can you get us out of here?"

"According to my calculations, Captain, we're rooted in place. I can determine no causal agent and, therefore, no solution."

Cut to Pluto

```
        H              H

    E      E      E        M  U

  H          H            A        S   E   D
```

Bonita Basset cupped her snout and called, "Dinner's ready! Come on, you guys, let's eat!"

Upstairs, in the rec room, Bill Basset sat in a hover-lounger watching his son track an earthship on the big-screen video-com.

"Look, Dad, they can't move!" cried Bobby gleefully. "Isn't that a riot?"

Bill Basset puffed on his pipe and smiled. "Son, Mom wants us down for dinner."

Bobby aimed his remote at the screen, pressed a button, and the earthship began rising and falling, like a pogo stick.

"Ha ha ha!" laughed Bobby.

"Heh heh," chuckled Bill.

"Bemused" is not a five-dollar version of "amused." "Bemused" means confused, bewildered. In the foregoing, Captain Jirk and his crew were "bemused" by the ship's inaction. On Pluto, Bill Basset (Get it? "Pluto—basset"?) was "amused" by Bobby's antics with the earthship.

Quick Quiz

Circle the correct choice(s) in each of the following:

1. The rookie on first was anxious and (bemused/amused) when the third base coach gave a sign the rookie had never seen before.
2. Blythe was totally (bemused/amused) when the repairman told her the "variable capacitor" had ruptured its "half-wave rectifier." All she knew was that the refrigerator had warmed up.
3. Mr. Klavin was not (bemused/amused) when little Finch raised his hand and said, "But if it's cloudy out, how do you *know* a sundial has the right time?"
4. Lady Hydrangea was (bemused/amused) when Giancarlo stopped the Mercedes, got out, and cried, "Do your own damn driving!"
5. After some guy in her court did an imitation of her, Queen Victoria glared at him and said, "We are not (bemused/amused)."

Answers

❶ **bemused** (The third base coach deliberately gave the rookie a sign he wouldn't understand because the third base coach had a cruel streak. When he gave up baseball, he became a book reviewer! (*Talk about asking for it!*))
❷ **bemused** (While the repairman was estimating the bill for Blythe, she noticed that the refrigerator was simply unplugged. Blythe then advised the repairman what he could do with his half-wave rectifier.)
❸ **amused** (Finch grew up to be a lawyer.)
❹ **bemused** (See, Lady? This is what happens when you try to be helpful, over and over and over and over again.)
❺ **amused** (Queen Victoria wasn't what you'd call a knee slapper.)

BOTTOM LINE: When you're b e m u s e d, you're muddled, mystified, mixed-up.

When you're a m u s e d, you're diverted, delighted, and some other "d" word that means "tickled."

Uninterested/

Disinterested

"How was the evening?"

"Awful." Greta kicked off her shoes and sighed. "He was a bore."

"Really? He seemed like such a nice boy."

"Then you date him, Ma."

"Don't get all worked up. What was so terrible about him?"

Greta groaned. "He kept asking me, 'Who would Dolly Parton be if she married Buddy Holly?' Then he'd blurt out, 'Dolly Holly!'"

"He asked that over and over?"

Greta shook her head. "He had others. 'Who would Liza Minnelli be if she married Paul Reiser? Who would Phyllis Diller be if she married Bruce Willis? Who would Whoopi Goldberg be if she married Lyle Lovett?' "

Greta's mother ruminated. "Liza Reiser, Phyllis Willis—but, Whoopi Lovett?"

Greta gestured. "He said, 'If Whoopi Goldberg married Lyle Lovett, she'd be making a big statement with her name: Whoopee! Love it!' "

Greta's mother chuckled. "Sounds to me as if Arlen has a sense of humor. Why not give him another chance? First impressions are—Greta, where are you going? Greta?"

Greta wasn't exactly holding out for a man with the mind of Mario Cuomo and the body of Fabio. She just wanted someone she felt comfortable with, someone she could talk to, someone who had the same interests, someone who was *interesting*.

Arlen bored her to tears. He was *uninteresting*. Greta was *uninterested* in him.

Greta's mother, on the other hand, was only interested in seeing Greta settle down. Therefore, Greta's mother had a special interest in any man Greta dated. (And you might, too, if you knew Greta better. She never did pick up her shoes.) Greta's mother was not an impartial judge. She was not *disinterested*.

"Uninterested" means unconcerned, not giving a damn; "disinterested" means not having an ax to grind or something to gain in any given situation; if you're "disinterested," you're objective, impartial, fair.

Examples

➤ Johnny Appleseed was *uninterested* in grapes. That's why he went around planting apple, not grape, seeds.
➤ "A Little League umpire is supposed to be *disinterested*," Mr. Bonilla declared as he grabbed Mr. Saberhagen by the collar. "You're supposed to call them as they are, even when your own son is pitching!"
➤ *Uninterested* in "mind candy," Hermione grabbed the re-

mote and turned off *All My Chilblains*, which her husband was watching.

➤ "Are you crazy?" cried the freshman senator, who hadn't gotten the hang of it yet. "We can't ask the guys from All-Four-Us Auto Repair to write the law regulating body shops. They're not *disinterested* parties!"

Quick Quiz

Circle the correct choice(s) in each of the following:

1. Bunnie Rocks sat through the opening night performance of *Iguana Go Home!*, even though she found it (uninteresting/disinteresting).
2. Drew Dunsimore raved about the show on local TV, but that's no surprise. The producer is never a(n) (uninterested/disinterested) critic.
3. Mrs. Dunsimore was (uninterested/disinterested) in what went on at the party that night—she was home with a cold—until she spotted Bunnie Rocks beside Drew on TV.
4. The judge was as (uninterested/disinterested) as he could be in the divorce case, considering his son was Mrs. Dunsimore's lawyer.

Answers

❶ **uninteresting** (Bunnie Rocks liked musicals or shows that had a lot of feathers in them.)
❷ **disinterested** (The truth is, Drew was more interested in fostering "personal relationships" than in producing good theater.)
❸ **uninterested** (It's amazing how quickly her health came back when she saw Bunny snuggling up to Drew.)
❹ **disinterested** (You and I could live very nicely for a lifetime on what Mrs. Dunsimore ended up getting.)

BOTTOM LINE: You're "uninterested" in hearing how electricity is produced in a thermal power plant. You're a "disinterested" judge of the best shade of blue for Bronia's contact lenses.

Alluding/ Eluding

"Allude to" means to refer indirectly to something or someone. "Elude" means to dodge danger or difficulty successfully.

Examples

➤ "Like Will Rogers, Dixie never met a man she didn't like," said Maude, *alluding* to Dixie's uninhibited social life.
➤ "Quick, in here!" cried Charlton. Fleeing into the museum's Etruscan galleries, he and Ursula managed to

elude Mr. Howser, who, with several tanks of salamanders, occupied the apartment above theirs.

➤ Anthony Hopkins's waiter chuckled and held his pen to his pad. "May I get you an order of liver with fava beans and a nice chianti?" he asked, alluding to Sir Anthony's role in *The Silence of the Lambs*. (Betcha *that* never happened before to Sir A. in all these years!)

➤ The fly kept eluding the swatter, so Mr. Schweitzer went for a can of bug spray.

BOTTOM LINE: Zora was unable to *elude* Brad any longer, once he cornered her in the patisserie. Plaintively, she said, "Brad, I think you're swell, but I can't marry you until you get that monkey off your back." Zora was not *alluding* to a problem with drugs; Brad actually went around with a capuchin monkey on his back.

Amount/ Number

Amount of	Number of
cement	mob hits
gold	medals, teeth
sugar	cubes, sweet nothings from Tad
photography	hazy views of Stonehenge
hot air	tiny ads for "ancient formulas" that cure baldness

Getting it?

fiction	promises from Tad not to do it again
inattention	stubbed toes
money	clams, smackeroos
coffee	trips to the john
communication	cries of "Hey, Bozo!"

This is fun!

insurance	large traveling companions named Carmine
risk	hours at the Sun-Yourself-Skinless-Salon
confusion	bureaucrats
despair	bureaucrats
irritability	bureaucrats

Okay, okay, I'll stop.

> **POINTED TIP:** Think in terms of "one lump" (the amount) and "individual lumpettes" (the number).

Quick Quiz

Circle the correct choice(s) in each of the following:

1. Sancho Panza sighed. "I wish I had a dollar for the (number/amount) of times Don Quixote stood in front of a windmill and yelled, 'Blow it out your ear!' "
2. "Do you believe the (number/amount) of carrot shakes Peter drinks?" said Mrs. Rabbit to Herr Hare. "I'm surprised he's not orange, given the (number/amount) of vitamin A in his system."
3. "I took one look at Medusa and just about turned to stone," confided Perseus. "You should have seen the (num-

ber/amount) of snakes on her head. I mean, talk about overkill."

4. From the (number/amount) of unbuttoned good cheer Trixie displayed at Orson's downsizing party, he concluded she'd had a fair (number/amount) of boilermakers.

5. "My name is Rifka Ravishing, and I need a huge (number/amount) of reassurance," cooed the blonde to Dr. Umlaut. Leaning forward, she added, breathily, "I've already seen a/an (number/amount) of shrinks, but they haven't been satisfactory. Can you accommodate me?"

6. "What with the (number/amount) of geysers and volcanoes erupting lately, the (number/amount) of tourism has fallen off, so I've moved back to Norway." That was what Angolfr Arnarsson scrawled on the rock outside his hut eighteen months or so after he founded Reykjavik, Iceland, in 874 A.D.

Answers

❶ **number** (You could always count on the Don for a few laughs!)

❷ **number, amount** (Peter did develop pinkeye.)

❸ **number** (A story went around, years back, that Medusa had snakes for hair and that anyone who looked at her was turned to stone. Radio psychologists—who hadn't seen her—theorized that she'd simply taken the moussed look too far, and that if you suddenly caught sight of her, you might just go rigid with shock for a minute. The truth is, she *did* have snakes on her head and really could turn passersby into bearing walls. Some say Perseus escaped this fate by keeping his right eye closed when he ran into her. Of course, his *left* side seized right up on him, but he used his right leg to take Medusa down with a kick in the asps.)

❹ **amount, number** (Orson really takes the cake. Talk about poor judgment! Lack of insight! Shortsightedness! Trixie was drinking Manhattans!)

❺ amount, number (Dr. Umlaut, who'd been studying Ms. Ravishing's chest as she was speaking—to make sure she wasn't hyperventilating—immediately cleared his desk, uh, calendar.)

❻ number, amount (You can still pretty much get a motel room there on short notice.)

BOTTOM LINE: The *amount* of time Hans Christian Andersen put into beautifying Ms. Ugly Duckling could be broken down into the *number* of hours she spent attending honking lessons and private styling sessions with Vidal Raccoon.

Irritate/

Aggravate

Vlad the Hypoglycemic had a really vexing time of it in 1130 A.D. First, he lost the hand of the Lady Vadka. He was pretty sure he had it on him when he was toppling the stone wall his slaves had just finished building. But the next morning, even though he left no stone unturned, Vlad couldn't find it for the life of him.

Then, when he decided to conquer the people beyond the mountain with the big hats (the people had the hats), his vassals said, "Forget it."

And *then* his favorite soothsayer fell under some kind of spell. For days, he went around shouting, "Who gets the veal cutlet?"

Vlad was one *irritated* hypoglycemic. What really *aggravated* matters, however, was not hearing from the great god Sucroscz after Vlad threw him that party (and seventeen contenders for the throne into the next time zone).

In the end, Vlad tossed his throne headfirst at the portcullis (that heavy, iron gate that comes down with a clang) and became a mendicant wayfarer. Actually, he didn't beg so much as borrow, and then, if you asked for your mace (the ball with spikes all over it) back, he'd grab you by your weskit (I'm not a dictionary) and wonder if you were so sure you'd lent it to him in the first place. (All right—"weskit" is how the English pronounce "waistcoat.")

Irritate: to annoy someone, bother me, get on my nerves.
Aggravate: to make a bad situation worse.

POINTED TIP: You can't aggravate someone; you only irritate him or her. You aggravate a condition or a situation or something like that.

Examples

➤ Wendell was *irritated* because the stationery store was out of medium refills for his favorite ballpoint pen.
➤ Paul Revere was *irritated* when the town fathers forgot to invite him to the Minute Men's picnic. The head of the festivities committee *aggravated* matters when he scribbled Paul's name on the list of honorees at the last minute, in pencil.

Simple enough, n'est-ce pas?

Quick Quiz

Circle the correct choice(s) in each of the following:

1. "Just because I take my time parallel parking doesn't mean I can't do it," Valerie muttered. She was (irritated/aggravated) at the way Vincenzo sat there, tsking,

as she tried for the tenth time to squeeze in between a Volkswagen and a hearse.

2. "Stop picking!" his mother cried. "You're only (irritating/aggravating) it!"

3. Priscilla, who read women's magazines, patiently explained to Monroe why she was divorcing him: "Your compulsion to leave cabinet doors ajar has been (irritating/aggravating) me for some time. And now that you're leaving your shoelaces undone as well, you're (irritating/aggravating) my sense of insecurity intolerably."

4. "If you scare them one more time, son," warned Mr. Kruger, "you'll (irritate/aggravate) things so much, you'll never get an invitation for New Year's."

5. Men with long fingernails who didn't play the guitar (irritated/aggravated) Miss Otis.

Answers

❶ **irritated** (Vincenzo was as pesky as a gnat sometimes.)

❷ **aggravating** (You don't want to know.)

❸ **irritating, aggravating** (Priscilla never did experience a sense of closure with Monroe.)

❹ **aggravate** (Mr. Kruger longed for Freddy to give him a daughter-in-law and grandghouls.)

❺ **irritated** (That might have been what led to her outburst with the gun, which caused Miss Otis to miss lunch that day.)

BOTTOM LINE: Your mother can't "aggravate" the life out of you. She can only "irritate" you to death. It's in the fine print.

Hysterical/
Hilarious

Hysterical:	Oh, my God! This can't be happening! Somebody, help! Aaaa-aaagh!!
Hilarious:	That's the funniest thing I ever heard! My stomach is killing me! Hahahahahaha!!

Quick Quiz

Now that you understand the distinction, fill in the following blanks with either "hysterical," "hilarious," "hysterically," "hilariously," "hysteria," or "hilarity":

1. Muddyman became _____ when he stepped outdoors for the morning paper and discovered a 40-foot alligator chewing Mrs. Muddyman's bathrobe.
2. "Personally," carped Andante, "I never found Bugs Bunny all that _____."
3. "Admittedly, I was on the verge of _____ when I encountered my first alien from outer space," declared Professor Mossback.
4. Crying _____ , Pockington tried to retrieve his scathing letter from the mailbox.
5. (George Carlin/Rosie O'Donnell/Stan Laurel/Jerry Lewis/Louie Anderson/Buddy Hackett/Phyllis Diller/Jerry Seinfeld/Oliver Hardy/Red Buttons/Ellen DeGeneres/Alan King/Jay Leno/Roseanne/George Burns/Steven Wright/Soupy Sales/David Letterman/Gracie Allen/Henny Youngman/Richard Lewis/Tim Allen/John Byner/Richard Pryor/Eddie Murphy/Charlie Chaplin, Jeff Foxworthy) is or was the most  comedian I've ever seen.
6. The used-computer salesman said, "I promise you this machine is in perfection condition," while, in the background, his partner rocked with _____.

Answers

❶ **hysterical** (Mr. Muddyman *loved* that robe!)

❷ **hilarious** (You should hear the rude noise Bugs makes when you bring up her name.)

❸ **hysteria** (But, you know, after a while, you brush right past 'em.)

❹ **hysterically** (Pockington had written to the IRS. You can now write to *him* care of Cellblock Seven, White Collar Pen.)

❺ **hilarious** (So, sue me. I left out Buster Keaton, Tommy Smothers, Harold Lloyd, Danny Thomas, Chris Rock, Robin Williams, Dana Carvey, Martin Short, Mort Sahl,

Dom DeLuise, Steve Martin, Wayne Newton, Robert Klein, and Jackie Whatsisname from junior high, who was such a sketch.)

⑥ hilarity (I swear, on my mother's head, the only person who owned this laptop was an eighty-year-old poet who suffered long periods of creative infertility.)

BOTTOM LINE: There's nothing *hilarious* about being *hysterical* (remember your first zit?).

Reticent/

Reluctant

Please. Don't confuse "reticent" with "reluctant." Here's "reticent" in action:

Mark, a young M.B.A. from Madison, Wisconsin, is vacationing on Cape Cod. It's June. Early one pleasant morning, he buys himself a cappuccino and parks himself down at the docks.

After watching the gulls for a while, he grows bored. He decides to strike up a conversation with an old man who's fishing off the pier.

MARK: "Nice morning."
OLD MAN: "Umm."

MARK (with a gesture): "You lived here long?"

OLD MAN: "Umm."

MARK (smiles): "I'm kind of surprised to see you fishing here, with all the boats."

OLD MAN: "Umm."

MARK: "I mean, I wouldn't think you'd get much." (He takes a breath and exhales.) "But, then, I guess that depends on what you're fishing for . . . I guess."

OLD MAN (scratches his cheek)

MARK (peers up at the sky): "Beautiful day. No sign of rain or anything. Guess I picked the perfect time for a visit."

OLD MAN: "Umm."

MARK (swinging his arms and backing away): "Well, have a good day."

OLD MAN: "Umm."

The old man is "reticent." *He's quiet, by nature.* You have to operate to get a word out of him. (Incidentally, don't go getting bent out of shape: Is the old man a stereotype? Yes. Are there hundreds of thousands of New Englanders who talk your ear off? *Yes.* Jeez.)

On the other hand, "reluctant" means "unwilling, grudging." But you know that. And now that you understand the difference between "reticent" and "reluctant," prove it:

Quick Quiz

Circle the correct choice(s) in each of the following:

1. When the Feds called Charlotte Russe to testify against her sweetie pie, Mussels Marinara, she was a (reluctant/reticent) witness.
2. My uncle Louis, who married "Miriam the Mouth," was the most (reluctant/reticent) man I ever knew.
3. Teddy was (reluctant/reticent) to tell Mr. Hayflick that, heh-heh, he'd "misplaced" Mr. Hayflick's Super Bowl tickets.

4. All things considered, you could say that Anthony Perkins's "mother" in *Psycho* was one (reluctant/reticent) lady!

5. Emil is (reluctant/reticent) to "open wide" and let the dentist probe his molar that's been throbbing for weeks.

6. If you want to do play-by-play announcing for the Central High Cantaloupes, you'd better not be (reticent/reluctant), or you'll be off the air in two minutes flat.

7. Madge was (reluctant/reticent) to let PunctureWound, the bald, tattooed hairdresser, cut her hair.

8. Your superego is never (reluctant/reticent) to tell you what's on its mind; one thing your superego is not is (reluctant/reticent).

Answers

❶ **reluctant** (Charlotte was no Rhodes Scholar, but she was no dummy, either.)

❷ **reticent** (Uncle Louis said "hello" and "good-bye." Aunt Miriam took care of everything in between.)

❸ **reluctant** (They don't call Arnold Hayflick the "shark of the toilet paper industry" for nothing, you know.)

❹ **reticent** (Perkins's mom was a *corpse*, remember?)

❺ **reluctant** (And *you'd* invite him in, I suppose!)

❻ **reticent** (If you're tight-lipped, how will we know what kind of season the Cantaloupes are having?)

❼ **reluctant** (Personally, I'd give PunctureWound a chance, but I've got a lot of guts.)

❽ **reluctant, reticent** (Your superego—that annoying voice in your head—is the first to remind you that every time you sit down, "Your thighs go splat, like pancake batter on a griddle!")

POINTED TIP: You can *never* combine "reticent" with "to," as in, "Hyacinth is reticent to do the hokey-pokey."

You can always be "reluctant to" eat headcheese,
or pay Cousin Leroy's long-distance bill.

BOTTOM LINE: "Reticent" means "quiet—from
dusk until dawn, year after year." "Reluctant" means
"I'd really rather not, so back off."

Jealous/

Envious

During her visit to the Galápagos Islands with Vernon, Vera noticed how often he ogled Bambie (especially when she bent over to fix little Richie's blanket). By the time they were back in Greenwich, Connecticut, Vera was shopping around for an older, larger-framed nannie.

Luigi tossed the pigs' guts into the street and sat down to take his morning break. Just then, Leonardo da Vinci passed by, carrying his plans for a flying machine. Luigi gave him a look and sniffed: "He thinks he's so smart."

What strikes you about this? Yes, Elva.
"Jealousy involves a rival. You fear you're being supplanted

by someone else. Envy is an unsatisfied longing for something someone else owns or can do or—"

That's enough, Elva. Don't push it.

In other words, you may be *envious* of Felicia's excellent posture, Diane Sawyer's salary, Victor Borge's or Dr. John's way with a piano, and/or the way Dick Van Dyke fell over that ottoman.

You may be *jealous* when a third party threatens to shake up your special relationship with

➤ Alec Baldwin or Kim Basinger (you wish)
➤ your best friend (you thought)
➤ your two-month-old beagle puppy, Bagel

So, Vera was jealous. She had the feeling Bambie was commandeering Vernon's affections. Luigi, on the other hand, was envious. He was ticked off that Leonardo didn't have to work with his hands for a living (well, not in slop, as Luigi did).

Quick Quiz

Circle the correct choice(s) in each of the following:

1. "Billy Ray Cyrus isn't so good-looking, and he's not much of a singer," said Jethro (enviously/jealously) as he scanned the personal ads.

2. When Eve raced off in a fit of (envy/jealousy), Adam ran after her crying, "I swear, honey, there's no one else!"

3. "You're just (envious/jealous) because I've got the touch and you haven't," said King Midas to his wife, who'd suddenly become fond of *silver* bangles.

4. Chuck was (envious/jealous) of the way Cliff could chat to him about women while executing complex financial transactions.

5. "Me, Tarzan. You, Jane," said Tarzan. Then, with a glint of (envy/jealousy) in his eye, he turned to the guy who resembled Tom Selleck. "And this is Walt, who runs the trading post. You have inventory to get to, don't you, Walt?"

6. Demi Tasse's evil stepmother was (envious/jealous) of how Demi always looked as if she'd been at Elizabeth Arden's when, in fact, she'd been pounding mattresses all day.

Answers

❶ **enviously** (Just so you know, Jethro didn't have anything good to say about any other man who dated regularly either.)

❷ **jealousy** (There's no one else! Get it?)

❸ **envious** (It's not always the little things that ruin relationships.)

❹ **envious** (Oops, Cliff just dropped another couple of zeroes. I'd find another stockbroker, if I were you.)

❺ **jealousy** (Tarzan had already been through this with Walt over a tour leader named Sheena.)

❻ **envious** (Plus which, Demi could stuff her mouth all day and still fit into a size three.)

BOTTOM LINE: If somebody has something you want, you're "envious." If somebody has, or is after, someone you want, you're "jealous." That's all perfectly normal despite what Dr. Umlaut says.

Accede/

Exceed

10 September 1849

Dear Mr. Dickens:

I beg to advise you that we are honored to reserve rooms in your name at our modest Humble Inn for the week of the twenty-third.

My poor wife and I shall be more than delighted to *accede to* any wish of yours while you are with us.

Should you desire an extra slop pot, say the word, and one of our unworthy children—we are blessed with twenty-seven!—will lug one to your room on his or her poor, spindly legs.

Should you require some fresh quill pens, with which to

work on one of your extraordinary tales, I myself shall hasten to the river and "de-quill" the largest, most ferocious goose I can find, whatever the risk to my own paltry well-being.

In short, my dear sir, my inferior family and I shall indeed do more than humanly possible to *exceed* your expectations of the hospitality awaiting you at our miserable lodgings.

Your most obedient servant,
U. Heep

15 September 1849

My dear Heep,
My obligation to my deadlines, alas, *exceeds* my wish to spend a few days of leisure in your accommodating company. I fear I must *accede to* my publisher's demands and cancel my stay at your Humble Inn. As amends, I am enclosing an advance copy of the next chapter of *David Copperfield*, which, I trust, you will enjoy.

As ever,
C. Dickens

"Exceed" means to surpass or go beyond the limit. "Accede" means to agree or consent to something, and is followed by "to." For instance:

➤ When driving with his wife, Mr. Spacey never *exceeded* the speed limit. On his own, he was an unguided missile.
➤ "I'll *accede* to your request for a raise," Halliburton told Ms. Miniver, leering, "if you *accede* to my, uh, requests."

Quick Quiz

Circle the correct choice(s) in each of the following:

1. "We can't get Alfie down from the ceiling, Doctor," said Mrs. Sandburg. "Could it be because we (acceded to / ex-

ceeded) your recommended dose of Warp-Time Tonic by 10,000 milligrams?"

2. "If you don't want to (accede to/exceed) my plans for amateur night, Mr. Christian," Captain Bligh said sharply, "then you can damn well get off my ship!"

3. Perry Winkle thought that announcing a movie's box office receipts on the news (acceded to/exceeded) the definition of "news" in a big way.

4. Dardanella was never able to master the art of weaving. Everything came out lopsided, because her woof always (acceded to/exceeded) her weft.

5. King Hrolf the Wuss always (acceded to/exceeded) his mother's commands, which was one reason the people fanned their noses at him when he rode through town.

6. This particular morning, Melley-Melley-Sweet-as-Jelly refused to (accede to/exceed) the subway conductor's warning to "watch the closing doors."

7. Hoyt (acceded to/exceeded) the racing world's highest hopes when he bred a horse that had eight legs.

8. "Why are you always trying to (accede to/exceed) Yvette's international investments?" cried Yves to his wife Yma.

Answers

❶ **exceeded** (Another 1,000 mg and Alfie would be orbiting Dubuque.)

❷ **accede to** (Captain Bligh always insisted on the same old parrot chorales.)

❸ **exceeded** (Whatever happened to the days when they just told you whether or not Siskel and Ebert *liked* the film? Why is it important for us to know what it grossed? Well?)

❹ **exceeded** (In other words, Dardanella's weft was worse than her . . . bite!)

❺ **acceded to** (They also thumbed their noses at Hrolf the Wuss because he was rather indifferent to personal hygiene.)

❻ accede to (Melley-Melley preferred to watch the guy who was having an animated discussion with thin air. She was dying to ask him, "When you go to the movies, do you buy *two* tickets?")

❼ exceeded (The only problem with the horse was that four legs always went left, while the other four turned right.)

❽ exceed (Ah, Yves! Yvette envies Yma's easy efficiency in issues economical.)

BOTTOM LINE: When Vachel *exceeded* (surpassed) his budget for "incidentals," he was obliged to *accede* (consent) *to* Mr. Lindsay's demand for a specific breakdown. Vachel had a hard time explaining how a pair of men's Gucci dress shoes fit the category.

Accede/Exceed

47

I Could

Care Less!

Lila's been seeing Fred for a month or so. Tonight, for the first time, they double-dated with Lila's best friend, Lydia, and her guy of the week.

Now Lila and Fred are parked outside Lila's house. She's sitting stiffly by the passenger door; he's slumped behind the steering wheel.

FRED: "You gonna tell me what's wrong?"

LILA (with a snort): "What makes you think something's wrong?"

FRED (sighing): "What, I danced with Lydia? You *told* me to!"

LILA (turning her blistering eyes on him): "Did I tell you to hold her so close* [*sic*] she was practically behind you?!"

FRED: "Hey, come on—"

LILA: "Forget it. I don't want to talk about it. If you want to behave like a pig, that's your business." She opens the car door, gets out, leans back in for an instant, and, before slamming the door, trumpets: "*I could care less!*"

What Lila *meant* was, "I have absolutely no interest—none—in how you pawed Lydia. It doesn't bother me at all!"

Unfortunately, that's not what she said.

Think about it. "I . . . *could* . . . care . . . less." If you finished the thought, it would be, "I could care less—*than I do now.*" Therefore, Lila indicated to Fred (the slimeball) that his behavior was actually driving her up the wall. And as for Lydia, that little snake . . .

Enough.

Lila should have said, "I *couldn't* (could *not*) care less!"

---

*Lila doesn't know yet that she needs an "ly" here. She will, after she reads "He Played Aggressive . . ."

BOTTOM LINE: When you want to skewer someone with a parting shot, let loose with "I *couldn't* care less," or "Hey! You're confusing me with someone who cares!"

All **T**ogether/

Altogether

All together, Mal, Merv, and Zel put up the money.
All together, Mal, Merv, and Zel signed an agreement.
All together, Mal, Merv, and Zel formed a company.
All together, Mal, Merv, and Zel rented space.
All together, Mal, Merv, and Zel hired employees.
All together, Mal, Merv, and Zel opened for business.
All together, Mal, Merv, and Zel started to fight.
All together, Mal, Merv, and Zel lost money.
All together, Mal, Merv, and Zel came to blows.

Separately, Mal, Merv, and Zel sued each other.

Altogether, it was a disaster.

Use "all together" when you mean a bunch of chameleons, clotheslines, whatever, all together at one time. Use "altogether" when you mean "completely, totally."

Quick Quiz

Circle the correct choice(s) in each of the following:

1. "We had an (altogether/all together) frightful time in the House of Horrors," said Marcelle with a wink.
2. General Knowledge was thrilled when he spotted his old troops (altogether/all together) behind the hedges.
3. Say you've got 4,637 apples, 517 pears, 9,002 pome-grantes, and 12 grapes. Put them (altogether/all together) and you get—
4. Lianne was (altogether/all together) humiliated when she blew her nose in the movie theater and accidentally honked.
5. The Tuckets never fought with Nan, unless they were cramped (altogether/all together) on a small island.
6. "What you're doing is (altogether/all together) a waste of time," Mrs. Einstein told Albert.

Answers

❶ **altogether** (Marcelle was a riot.)
❷ **all together** (It was just like old times for the general!)
❸ **all together** (Fruit cup for Staten Island.)
❹ **altogether** (Just Lianne's luck, she honked when the teenage heroine was calling, "Warren?" and tiptoeing into the festive but poorly lighted crypt.)
❺ **all together** (Quit crowding me!)
❻ **altogether** (Relatively speaking, Mrs. Einstein was a buttinsky of the first order.)

BOTTOM LINE: "When The Beatles were *all to-gether*," said Alexa sweetly, "my hair was *altogether* brown." Then, grabbing a fistful of gray hair, she began to sob.

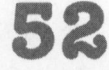

Infer/

Imply

Noon. A dark and gloomy day in the forest. The animals are gathered around a clearing. It is the second day of the trial of Chicken Little, accused of causing havoc by crying, "The sky is falling!"

"Court is in session. Proceed, Counselor."

"Thank you, Judge Lurkey." Foxy Loxy approaches the witness. "Yesterday, Henny Penny, you said—and I quote—'Ever since he was a little chick and broke out of his shell, Chicken Little has been, you know . . .' Then, you pointed at your temple and made a circular motion with your, uh, foot, finger, whatever that is. Is that correct?"

"Yes."

"And, by that, I believe you meant that Mr. Little has always been 'nuts.' "

"Objection!" Ducky Wucky ruffles her feathers. "The prosecution is *inferring* that Henny Penny thinks my client is bananas!"

Foxy Loxy bares his teeth in a smile. "Yes—because that's exactly what she was *implying*!"

"Order!" Judge Lurkey shakes his wattle and turns to Henny Penny. "Ms. Penny, is Foxy Loxy's *inference* about your *implication* accurate?"

Henny Penny puts her, uh, foot, finger, whatever that is, to her head. A strained look crosses her face. "I've got a splitting headache. I'm going to lie down now."

Who can blame Henny? Infer, imply. What's the difference? *Imply*: to hint, to suggest; *infer*: to gather a meaning from or draw a conclusion about something (or someone).

Examples

➤ From the way Mr. Carmichael coughed and waved his hands whenever Marlene lit a menthol-light, she *inferred* (concluded) that he was put out by her smoking.

➤ "Do you really need that?" Jerome said as Janine drizzled fudge over her pound cake. Obviously, he was *implying* (suggesting) she was already as big as a house.

➤ *Implying* (suggesting) that he wanted to buy off the mayor, the developer pushed the unmarked envelope to the mayor's side of the table.

➤ *Inferring* (concluding) that the developer was trying to buy him off, the mayor pocketed the envelope. "I don't see *why* we shouldn't tear down the foundling hospital and build a casino!" he said, grinning.

Now, read the courtroom scene again and substitute "suggest" for "imply," and "conclude" for "infer."

Quick Quiz

Circle the correct choice(s) in each of the following:

1. After Sylvia admitted to singing along with "Don't Cry for Me, Argentina" in the supermarket, Dr. Umlaut sighed. And Sylvia (implied/inferred) that she *wasn't* progressing after all.

2. Bruno always squinted at her when she sashayed over to the Xerox machine, so Cookie (implied/inferred) that he thought she was some dish.

3. "By the way, have you seen my diamond cuff links?" Donald asked. "Are you (inferring/implying) I'm a thieving fortune hunter?" Marlo responded.

4. "You're supposed to *wash* shrimp before frying them?" Adrienne said sheepishly. Claude, (implying/inferring) that she hadn't, put down his fork.

5. Monroe headed for the "self-help" shelves in Barnes & Noble. Clarissa, who was watching him, (inferred/implied) that he was a fellow neurotic and sidled up to him.

6. "It's important that *you* like wrought-iron chairs in the living room," cooed Marlene's mother, (implying/inferring) that Marlene was no Maurice Villency.

Answers

❶ **inferred** (concluded) (Sylvia was always quick to assume she was falling short of Dr. Umlaut's expectations. She *so* wanted to please him.)

❷ **inferred** (concluded) (Actually, Bruno was nearsighted and had a lot of copying to do. Cookie, however, didn't suffer from Sylvia's paralyzing lack of self-esteem. She made flattering interpretations of neutral situations all the time.)

❸ **implying** (hinting) (Uh-oh. Dinner and dancing tonight at the Plaza won't be much fun for *these* two!)

❹ inferring (concluding) (Hey, Adrienne majored in computer sciences, not good housekeeping. How's she supposed to know about shrimp?)

❺ inferred (concluded) (See, it really doesn't pay to jump to conclusions. Actually, Monroe's an author, checking out the market for yet another book on self-love, growth, and fulfillment—which Clarissa will surely buy.)

❻ implying (suggesting) (Marlene has her first appointment with Dr. Umlaut next week. Soon, Mummy, she'll be sticking it to you with wrought-iron furniture all over the place!)

POINTED TIP: Sherlock Holmes usually solved crimes through "inferences," based on the tiniest clues: "But how do you *know* the murderer is a heavyset man from Liverpool with whimsical tastes?" asked Watson. "From a heelprint bearing a 'drakes and ducks' pattern at the scene of the crime," said Holmes. "Only one firm—in Liverpool—specializes in footwear of this sort, for portly, lighthearted men!"

BOTTOM LINE: For "imply," imagine an English butler holding his nose while serving the cook's meatloaf. (They once had a thing, but she dumped him.) For "infer," picture Sherlock Holmes bent over a heelprint in the mud.

Bring/

Take

"Take me to your leader."
"Bring me back a beer."
"Take" goes out, away from you.
"Bring" comes home, back here.

"Take" has a million other meanings, but we're not concerned here with "take a number, take a gander, take sides," etc. We're just interested in "take"'s relationship to "bring."

Examples

➤ "He *brought* me the loveliest assortment of guitar picks," said Wynonna, eyes shining.
➤ "*Take* these maps to Columbus," Ferdinand told Isabella. "I'm not convinced he knows where he's going."

➤ "When you have a minute," called Humpty Dumpty, "*bring* me a stepladder!"

➤ Peter Minuit sipped his beer. "And then he said, '*Take* another twelve beads to the chief, and you've bought yourself an island.' " The barkeep nodded. "Sounds like a good deal to me."

Very Quick Quiz

Circle the correct choice(s) in each of the following:

1. "After you (take/bring) the mail to Kansas City a few times, we'll see about increasing your territory," the office manager told the new Pony Express rider.
2. "Waiter," cried Alberto, "(bring/take) me their checks, too! It's all on me, tonight!"

Answers

❶ **take** ("By the way," the office manager added, "what do you know about camels? We're thinking about expanding the line.")

❷ **bring** (What a guy! Too bad he's using a stolen credit card.)

BOTTOM LINE: Moira "takes" away your deviled eggs; Vaughn "brings" them back again.

Fewer/

Less

"Don't jaw at me about *less* work,"
Bar-B-Que Rue warned her dawdling clerk.
"Clean more tomatoes, instead of *fewer*,
Or I'll run you through with a ke-bab skewer!"

Hey, bully bully!
Strawberry tarts!
Use "less" for a "whole,"
And "fewer" for its "parts"!

Examples

Fewer	Less
piggies	ham
calendars	time
witches and warlocks	sorcery
kisses	love
hard knocks	education
earthquakes	upheaval
rumors	history
pitbulls	panic
raised eyebrows	disbelief
watts	light
octopuses	ink
revolving doors	running around in circles
rhinestones	glitz
onions and red peppers	heartburn

POINTED TIP: People do say, "With *less than fifty dollars* down, you can buy your own personalized rifle!" and *"In less than six weeks*, you, too, can learn to take down conspirators with one shot!"

That's because we don't break down "fifty dollars" into "dollar, dollar, dollar, dollar . . ." or "six weeks" into "week, week, week . . ." "Fifty dollars" is an amount of money; "six weeks" is an amount of time.

Quick Quiz

Circle the correct choice(s) in each of the following:

1. A charging elephant runs approximately 25 mph, which is 45 miles (fewer/less) than the cheetah runs in an hour.

2. In Alaska, the county of Skagway-Yakutat-Angoon has (fewer/less) people per square mile—0.3—than the county of Aleutians East (0.4).

3. "If you devoted (fewer/less) time to O.T.B.," Manny's mother scolded him, "you'd have (fewer/less) headaches!"

4. Biff had (fewer/less) T-shirts, shoes, belts, and blazers than Page, which meant that he took up (fewer/less) space in the closet.

5. The Louis-Hippolyte Lafontaine Tunnel in Montreal has (fewer/less) feet than the Lincoln Tunnel in New York City: 5,280 vs. 8,216 ft. Therefore, you may spend (fewer/less) time underwater in Montreal than in New York.

6. There are (fewer/less) cars in Micronesia than in Mesa, Arizona, which means there is (fewer/less) traffic there, too.

7. "But enough about me," said Cora ebulliently. "What do you think about me?" She was addressing Ginger, who had (fewer/less) ego and, therefore, (fewer/less) self-portraits.

8. "Someday, when there's (fewer/less) unemployment," said the new secretary of labor, "there'll be (fewer/less) people out of work!"

9. "I just wish there were (fewer/less) grope-and-slobber shows on TV," complained Carlton. "I'd like to see (fewer/less) violence there, too."

10. Chile's flag has (fewer/less) blue than the USA's, and (fewer/less) stars.

Answers

1 **fewer** (Is the guy who timed these speed demons out of traction yet?)

2 **fewer** (That makes Skagway-Yakutat-Angoon County the ideal vacation spot for hermits.)

3 **less, fewer** (Manny's mother meant that remark about "headaches" literally. Manny was always explaining to men with callused knuckles that, ouch!, he'd have the money in "just a couple of more days, heh heh.")

4 **fewer, less** (After Page threw Biff out, he took up no space at all.)

5 **fewer, less** (Hey, just because tunnels don't bother you doesn't mean somebody out there doesn't appreciate the information!)

6 **fewer, less** (Yes, but can you drive to an air-conditioned mall in Micronesia on a sultry afternoon?)

7 **less, fewer** (Ginger did have a photo of herself, taken when she and Cora were on vacation in Rome, but she kept it hidden in a drawer. It only reminded her that Cora had had a terrific time with a waiter named Cesare, while Ginger had seen a lot of art.)

8 **less, fewer** (Duh.)

9 **fewer, less** (Carlton no longer abided by "sex and violence sell," not since every suit in the industry rejected his teleplay, "Valentines for the Marquis de Sade."

10 **less, fewer** (Chile's flag has only one star.)

BOTTOM LINE: Use "fewer" for separate, individual things, and "less" for other stuff: Want fewer bills? Open less mail.

Compose/

Comprise

"Sherman's virtues were composed of good hygiene, excellent spelling, and faultless recall of Vinny Testaverde's football career."

"Sherman's vices comprised tap dancing with his teeth and taking every opportunity to show off what a good speller he was and how much he knew about Vinny Testaverde."

"The Midwest is composed of states in the middle of the country."

"The Midwest comprises those states that most Easterners cannot locate on the map."

From this, we can conclude that one word stands between "compose" and "comprise":

You

    can

        never

           say

               "*comprised of.*"

You

    must

        always

           say

               "*composed of.*"

POINTED TIP: "Comprise" is almost the same as "include," and you wouldn't say, "include of," now, would you? Of course not.

Examples

➤ Miss Americas from 1972 to 1974 *comprise* Laurie Lea Schaefer, Terry Anne Meeuwsen, and Rebecca Ann King.

➤ The group ABBA was *composed of* Bjorn Ulvaeus, Benny Andersson, Agnetha Faltskog, and Anni-Frid Lyngstad.

➤ A shopping list for Siberian tigers might *comprise* brisket, rib roast, veal cutlets, and fries.

➤ Sherman's ideal vacation is *composed of* two weeks in the rain forest, studying the habits of the incorrigible nudnick.

As you know, "compose" can also mean to make up something: Duffie *composed* a cantata in tribute to Grover Cleveland, while Daphne *composed* a letter to the Consumer Affairs Bureau regarding bait-and-switch tactics at Minnie's Mattress Outlet. And you can "compose," or "calm" yourself, in anticipation of the Rodney Dangerfield retrospective.

BOTTOM LINE: The alderman's constituency *comprised* blackguards, ne'er-do-wells, and brigands, which means it was *composed of* citizens who shared his big-fish-eat-little-fish-and-I-ain't-no-damn-smelt philosophy.

Continual/ Continuous

"Can Alexander come out and play, Mrs. Bell?" She smiled down at him. "I'm sorry, Tommy, he's working on his talking machine again."

Tommy frowned. "Gee, Mrs. Bell, he's *always* busy with that thing!"

Mrs. Bell knelt down and touched Tommy's shoulder. "Not always, not *continuously*," she said. "Alexander works on it off and on. *Continually*."

"More than that!"

"Well, maybe so, but that doesn't mean Alexander doesn't like you anymore, Tommy. You know that, don't you?"

Tommy thought for a moment. "Mrs. Bell?"

"Yes?"

"Would you give Alexander a message for me?"

"Of course."

"Tell him I'm going home to figure out how to make . . . to make"—his eye fell on the gaslight near the door—"to make a lamp that doesn't need gas. I'm going to make a better one!"

Mrs. Bell laughed softly. "Fine, Tommy Edison, I'll tell him." As Tommy darted down the path, Mrs. Bell watched him, shaking her head. "Loser," she muttered and went back into the house.

Remember it this way:

continual continual continual continual continual *(off and on, frequently)*

continuouscontinuouscontinuouscontinuouscontinuouscontinuouscontinuous *(nonstop)*

Quick **Q**uiz

Circle the correct choice(s) in each of the following:

1. "Isn't it true, Mr. Pabarotti, that you killed Mr. Rhapsido Flomingo because he parked his Alfa Romeo outside your house, and the car alarm rang (continually/continuously) all night long?"

2. "I married Thaddeus because he (continually/continuously) praised my eyebrows," remarked Arlette.

3. "I divorced Thaddeus because he (continually/continuously) snored," remarked Arlette.

4. Bicky made it into the book of records by (continually/continuously) shopping for 72 hours 13 minutes 04 seconds.

5. Mr. Silken stopped going to meditation class because the man with the harmonica was (continually/continuously) breaking into "Besame Mucho," and the (continual/con-

tinuous) pursuit of not thinking was giving Mr. Silken cramps.

6. The month before the bagpipe festival, Ilana had (continual/continuous) nightmares about losing her breath.

7. "Stop denying it, Samuel," said Mark Twain. "Your mother (continually/continuously) implies I'm not a good enough alias for you."

8. There was (continual/continuous) rain for three days straight when Janiger was in Morocco.

9. "Hi, Larry, thanks for taking my call. First, I want to say you seem to (continually/continuously) cut people off the air, and I—"

10. Mangrove the Magician had a messy studio because he (continually/continuously) spilled his bags of tricks.

Answers

❶ **continuously** (Tenors can be so temperamental.)

❷ **continually** (Arlette took pride in how she could express herself through her eyebrows.)

❸ **continually** (Six, seven times a night, Thaddeus would erupt, depriving Arlette of sleep. Consequently, she found her eyebrows twitching every which way.)

❹ **continuously** (Bicky developed "signature-ligature syndrome" from signing so many charge slips, but, hey, she's a champ!)

❺ **continually, continuous** (Eight bars of "Besame Mucho" every ten minutes go a long way.)

❻ **continual** (For Ilana, "windbag" had a whole other meaning.)

❼ **continually** (Relatives.)

❽ **continuous** (Not for nothing, but Moroccans called Janiger "rain man.")

❾ **continually** (What can I say? Some talk show hosts lack basic good man—)

❿ **continually** (Mangrove was known for his plight of hand!)

BOTTOM LINE: At first, Linus hummed *continually* (frequently), which was annoying but tolerable. When he began humming *continuously* (nonstop), however, the chess club threw him out.

Rear/
Raise

Y ou *raise* marigolds, long-haired dachshunds, flags, doubts, the dead, a glass to your lips, cain, the volume, your eyebrows, a call to arms, all kinds of hell, troops, lids, hats, suspicions, false hope, money, the fishing pole, a ruckus, one hip, a stink, your nose, objections, a hue and cry, a glass of lemonade, the other hip, a snifter of brandy, the rent, the stakes, the ante, the roof, your right hand, the possibility, the distinction, your average in biology, and that "stat" thing that makes the room warmer. . . .

You *rear* children.

BOTTOM LINE: You "rear" children and "raise" everything else under the sun.

Between/
Among

Head high, Gilbert was striding toward Mr. Furbelow's office when Flo, the office manager, stopped him. "Just *between* the two of us," she said in a hushed voice, "you're better off confronting him after he's knocked back a few beers at lunch." She patted Gilbert's arm. "Come back between three and four, dear— so you don't wind up between jobs."

Down *among* the sweltering palms, Auntie Ta-Ta finished chiseling her coconut-head likeness of Dan Rather. She studied it a moment. Satisfied, she set it down behind Peter Jennings, Tom Brokaw, and Hugh Downs.

Among primitive art connoisseurs, Auntie Ta-Ta was considered a peach. No one else had her touch. Her eye. Her recipe for macaroons. She checked her Rolex. Good. Uncle Ha-Ha would be back soon with the estimate of heads the big hotels wanted for tomorrow's merrymaking. Savoring the breeze off the lagoon, Auntie Ta-Ta smiled; *among* all the summer festivals celebrated on the island, the Carnival of Ph.D.s was her favorite.

"Between" is always—and *only*—used just between two things:

➤ between the two of us, the two of you, the two of them
➤ between Peter—and Paulie and Mary, who've had it up to here with that magic dragon
➤ between Abbott and Costello (an old comedy team) and Smith and Dale (an ancient comedy team)
➤ between Kukla, Fran, and Ollie (a trio) and Gladys Knight and her, what, three Pips, four?
➤ between hell and high water, between these and those, between a rock and a hard place.

"Among" is used among three and all the rest.

Very Quick Quiz

Circle the correct choice(s) in each of the following:

1. (Between/Among) Marco Polo's most prized souvenirs was a silver spaghetti twirler from China engraved, "Made in Taiwan."
2. Elihu had a hard time deciding (between/among) "Thanksgiving with the Lennon Sisters" and "The Osmond Brothers Sing a Hit."

Answers

❶ **among** (If they'd had UPS in those days, he'd have sent back a ton of them.)

❷ **between** (Elihu is a good boy. Would there were more like him in this cockeyed world.)

POINTED TIP: Never, ever say "between Larry, Moe, and Curly." It's "People always have a hard time deciding who was the most intellectual *among* Larry, Moe, and Curly."

BOTTOM LINE: Flo and Auntie Ta-Ta hit the nail on the head: It's always "just *between* two" and "*among* three or more."

Besides/

Beside

B
E
S
BESIDES = + *(plus, in addition to)*
D
E
S

beside/next to/beside/next to/beside/next to/beside

Besides Candie, Lauralee, and Bethesda, Lila wanted Madame Celeste to be one of her bridesmaids, if Fred ever proposed (assuming he even called again).

Fortunately, Katrina was standing *beside* Morgan when the chambermaid burst in with the mints.

BOTTOM LINE: There isn't anything else I can say, *besides* what I've already said, to illustrate the difference between *besides* and *beside*—except: Think of *beside* as another form of "by the side of."

Anx**iou**s/

Eager

"**H**ave a seat, Mr. Piper. What can I do for you?" Dr. Putznagle folded his hands and eyed the nervous little man, who was sitting on the powerless side of the Chippendale desk.

"I'm rather concerned," Mr. Piper said. Tentatively, he displayed his hands.

"Yiiccch! How long have you had that disgusting rash?"

Mr. Piper jammed his hands into his pockets and flushed. "A few weeks."

Putznagle tucked his own hands behind his back. "I imagine you're *anxious* to be rid of it. I sure as hell would be, heh heh!"

Mr. Piper nodded. "*Eager*, yes. And I am *anxious* about whether this might lead to something more serious."

The doctor rose. "More serious?" He backed his chair against the wall. "My God, man! *This* is no roll in the hay! I've got degrees up the wazoo, and I don't have an inkling what's behind your hideous condition."

"Well, I suspect it's my job."

The doctor folded his arms across his cashmere vest. "Uh-huh. And what is it you do?"

"I pick pickled peppers."

The doctor smiled.

"No, truly. And ever since they discovered that the red ones cure wrinkles, we've been working double shifts and—"

Dr. Putznagle gestured toward the door. "I'd love to hear more, Mr. Piper, but I've got to see a dying patient about a bill."

Anxiously, Mr. Piper regarded Putznagle. "Isn't there anything you can tell me?" he pleaded as the doctor shooed him out.

Eagerly closing the door on him, Putznagle replied, "We take cash or credit cards, no checks."

To the medical community: Hey, where's your sense of humor? The foregoing was simply a fiction to demonstrate that

"Anxious" means fearful, worried, nervous—whereas—
"Eager" indicates, Boy oh boy! am I looking forward to this!

To put it another way: "Anxious" is related to anxiety; "eager" is related to Beaver, on his mother's side.

Quick Quiz

Circle the correct choice(s) in each of the following:

1. The rumor that the English were coming made Betsy Ross so (anxious/eager), she sat up all night sewing.
2. Miss Florine eyed Raoul (anxiously/eagerly). "They call this a Pullman kitchen," she said, "which is really all a

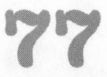

young bachelor like you needs in an apartment, don't you agree?"

3. "Okay, Phil, don't move." (Eagerly/Anxiously) William Tell took aim, while Phil (eagerly/anxiously) cast about for a door marked "Feet, don't fail me now."

4. Napoleon wasn't (anxious/eager) to conquer the world because he was (anxious/eager) about his height. It was all his therapist's idea.

Answers

❶ **anxious** (She was so upset, in fact, she only stitched thirteen stars and stripes.)

❷ **anxiously or eagerly** (Miss Florine had been trying to unload this overpriced two-by-nothing ever since she'd gotten her real estate license, so she was *eager* for Raoul to take it, and *anxious* that he wouldn't.)

❸ **eagerly, anxiously** (No, his son's name wasn't "Phil." "Phil" was a hitchhiker Mr. Tell happened to spot on the thruway.)

❹ **eager, anxious** (Josephine's tastes didn't exactly run to three-for-a-dollar.)

BOTTOM LINE: If you can't wait to skip through the Borneo jungle, you're "eager." If all you can think about are deadly snakes falling out of trees onto your head, you're "anxious," and right on the money, as far as I'm concerned.

Tenet/

Tenant

A tenant who paid his rent too late
Was hauled into court by his landlord irate.
Said the judge, "Why do you do it?"
Said the tenant, "Maybe someday, I'll rue it.
But paying on time for a seedy "to-let"
Violates my dearest, most precious *ten*et.

To wit: If this slimeball landlord doesn't replace my toilet, put lights in the hall, and fix the elevator, he can take me to court every day of the week before he sees a dime of mine on time!

As you can see: A *tenant* is a person who rents a room, an apartment, a place where he or she lives or works—an occupant; a *tenet* is a strong belief or opinion.

BOTTOM LINE: Newton's destitute mother was a *tenant* in one of his buildings. When he approved a 40 percent increase in her rent, he was applying his favorite *tenet*: "When money is involved, everything else goes out the window. And money is always involved!"

Enhancement/ Inducement

riends, if your life is cluttered with ruts and ditches, if you are confronted at every turn with:

Stop!

Slow!

Toll ahead!

Dangerous curve!

Yield right of way!

Lane ends!

No U-turn!

Merge!

Spiritual Speedways can rid you of these frustrating road-blocks! We can teach you how to avoid emotional wrong turns and traffic jams, and how to outrun any "truancy troopers" out to confiscate your license to cruise.

Join us on an exciting journey of self-realization. Call 1-800-HYPE, for your free Spiritual Speedways' "Short-Cuts to Paradise."

The foregoing was an "inducement" to "enhance" your life—and the pockets of Spiritual Speedways.

To "induce" means to lead you to do something, to persuade, to influence. ("Inducing" labor is a persuasion of another sort.)

To "enhance" means to make something more valuable, more attractive, more get-a-load-of-me.

Quick **Q**uiz

Circle the correct choice(s) in each of the following:

1. To (enhance/induce) his desirability and (enhance/induce) Mona to view him with lust in her heart, Kirby began using a facial cream called Stud Scrub.
2. In *The Taming of the Shrew*, Petruchio (enhanced/induced) Kate to become a docile wife by pushing her around.
3. "But, Mom, I *need* a cellular phone to (enhance/induce) my position with the guys!" cried E.T.
4. Dracula found that a quick bite on the neck was all it took to (enhance/induce) recruits to join his team.
5. Hilda was (enhanced/induced) to spend $75 on a "cat"sultation with Miss Leonine, animal behaviorist, after Marshmallow began scorning the Kitty-Litter box.
6. Those mysterious lines that (enhance/induce) the Nasca desert in Peru sometimes (enhance/induce) the idea of visits by extraterrestrials.

Answers

❶ enhance, induce (Mona spurned him anyway and joined a group of celibate evolutionists.)

❷ induced (I'd like to see the big "P" try that today!)

❸ enhance (Go fight peer pressure.)

❹ induce (Incidentally, Dracula's team colors were black and blue.)

❺ induced (Miss Leonine, a.k.a. Fern Rapscallion, had a nice thing going for herself. The "cat"sultation took place over the phone: Hilda held her cordless phone to Marshmallow's ear, and Miss Leonine "read" his vibrations on the other end.)

❻ enhance, enhance or induce (I, personally, don't believe a spaceship from Neptune hovered over Peru while one little Neptunaut elbowed the other and said, "Let's doodle some really big things in the desert down there—and leave without signing them!")

BOTTOM LINE: To *"enhance"* (add value to) his position as head of the community, Mr. Corleone *"induced"* (persuaded) others to support him by making them offers they couldn't refuse.

Enhancement/Inducement

Affect/
Effect

Take a Letter

"**D**agg, Hammershuld and Company, good morning. How may I direct your call?"

"Good morning, Hester."

"Hi, Mr. Dagg. Violet left your messages with me. Should I read them to you?"

"No, but I do need a favor."

"Sure."

"Take a letter for me, please."

"Where?"

"I mean I want to dictate a letter to you; then I want you to fax it."

"Sure."

"It's to Mrs. —"

"Hold on, let me get a pencil. Okay, shoot."

"To Mrs. Beryl Finger. Her number's on file.

"Dear Beryl,

Re: our meeting of the tenth and the advisability of pursuing a libel action against Opal Foote, I must advise you that the effect of such an action would be to adversely affect your standing in the hot tub industry, not to mention your personal relations with all the Footes. Nevertheless, if you wish to proceed with said action, please advise immediately, and I shall move ahead on receipt of your fax.

Yours sincerely, blah, blah, blah.

"Did you get that, Hester?"

"Yes, Mr. Dagg."

"Good. Send it out as soon as you can."

Hester sent the following fax:

Dear Barrel,

Ray R. meeting in the tent, and the advizabillaty of pursueing a lyeball aktion against oplefoot, I must advize you that the effect of sutch an aktion wood be to advurceally affect your Stan Ding in the hott tubb industree, not to menshun your pursunel relayshuns width all the feet.* Nevertheles, if you wisch to proseed width sed aktion, pleaze advize imediutly and I shall move a hed on recete of your facts.

Yourz sinceerly,
Blah, Blah, Blah.

No one is wrong all the time. Hester knew how to use "affect" and "effect."

*"Foots" just didn't sound right to Hester.

"*Affect*"—to have an influence upon something or someone.
"*Effect*"—the *result* of some action, the consequence.

Examples

➤ "What you do with your life won't *affect* me in the least," lied Vivienne. "Go ahead and give up otolaryngology for the bassoon, Pietro. I'll stand by you."

➤ Buttercup discovered that substituting black olives for chocolate chips had a vile *effect* on Fanny Farmer's recipe for fudge cookies.

POINTED TIP: "Affect" can also mean to pretend and to take on airs, as in, "Wilma *affected* the manner of a woman of means, when, in fact, she didn't have a pot to . . ." And "effect" can mean to *bring* about a result, as in, "Holly *effected* a bizarre change in the atmosphere of the sorority house by painting the hallways plaid."

Quick Quiz

Circle the correct choice(s) in each of the following:

1. "Vivaldi has no (affect/effect) on me," the lion told the DJ. Then he ate him.

2. Copernicus came up with the idea that we revolve around the sun, rather than vice versa. That had a severe (affect/effect) on his popularity; invitations to bread-and-cheese tastings dropped off.

3. Mr. Adolph lectured the residents of the Carefree-Living Condominiums on how a baseball's seams (affect/effect) the ball's flight through the air.

4. The (affect/effect) on Marisa of seeing Pierce cutting his nails on the bus was devastating. It (affected/effected)

her opinion of him in every way, from prospective spouse to valued numerologist.

5. "The best way to (affect/effect) a positive response from your clients," said Harrison, addressing the Time Savers' seminar, "is not to dwell on things. Don't keep saying the same thing over and over, in different words. Be brief. Concise. Don't go on and on. Make your point and get off. Vamoose. Scram. . . ."

6. Being bitten by a black widow spider will not have a good (affect/effect) on your opinion of female arachnids.

7. "Michael Feinstein has greatly (affected/effected) my taste in music," revealed Lauren. "I'm now listening to Rodgers and Hart, along with Salt-N-Pepa."

8. "Cause and (affect/effect)" is another way of saying, "You nodded off, and the clam chowder boiled over!"

9. The approach of autumn always (affects/effects) Mr. Montana the same way.

10. "I'm not going to argue with you," shouted Marigold. "Moonwort tea is *not* having a good (affect/effect) on your hearing!"

Answers

❶ **effect** (If the DJ had been playing Wynton Marsalis, he wouldn't have ended up decomposing in the lion's gastric juices. That cat loved jazz!)

❷ **effect** (Good thing; Copernicus was becoming lactose intolerant.)

❸ **affect** (It took the entire Carefree-Living Security Force to stop the audience from throwing their bifocals at Mr. Adolph. You see, his lecture was entitled "Seams in Time," and the audience—mainly women—had expected to learn about preventive sewing techniques.)

❹ **effect, affected** (It turned out that that wasn't all Pierce did in public. People can be such animals.)

⑤ effect (Here it is: "effect," as in to cause or bring about something, to generate a reaction, to make something happen.)

⑥ effect (You know what? Female arachnids don't give a fig what we think. Their boyfriends don't either.)

⑦ affected (Lauren's nana cried with thankfulness when she heard that.)

⑧ effect (Your father and I ask you to do one little thing, and what happens? It's not as if we asked you to wash the clams, dice the carrots, and boil the water. Watch the pot! Watch the pot! What does it take to WATCH THE POT?)

⑨ affects (Come late August, Mr. Montana has visions of pigtails . . . scratch that—pigskins.)

⑩ effect (Hawkeye cupped his ear and said, "What?")

BOTTOM LINE: The "pea under the mattress" had no *effect* on the busloads of girls who stayed over at the Winterhalter Palace. It didn't *affect* Gizelle, the upstairs maid, either. But she was so *affected*, saying "cahn't" and acting as if she never blew her nose, that the Winterhalters allowed Prince Figgy to take her as his wife anyway, which *effected* a change in the laws of ascendancy to the throne. They gave up the pea as a test of royalty and relied instead on "attitude."

Corps/

Corpse

"C orps" is pronounced "core," but the "p" and the "s" are pronounced in "corpse." Both words have to do with "body."

The Marine Corps is a group—or body—of soldiers. You can also have a "corps" of just about anyone else: butchers, ballet dancers, or bookkeepers.

A "corpse," though, is anyone who has "kicked the bucket," "met his maker," or enjoyed his last stack of silver dollars at IHOP. That's about it.

BOTTOM LINE: Use "corps" when you mean a body or group of people. Use "corpse" when you mean one dead dude.

Loath/

Loathe

"This happened on a Thursday in ancient Sumeria, a really long time ago. 'I hast been doing the monthly accounts for the king and hath lost track,' a baker told his wife. 'Wilt thou count the tablets inscribed so far?'

" 'I wilt,' said his wife, and off she went to the backyard. Several wet clay tablets, which were inscribed with wedgelike marks, were drying in the sun. The wife began counting them: 'One, two, three, five, six . . .' She reentered the workroom. 'There are thirteen tablets drying in the sun,' she told her husband.

" 'Hm,' he said, 'I thought there were twelve. Art you sure?'

"The wife rolled her eyes. 'I wilt check again.'

"This time, she counted correctly. But, *loath* to tell her husband that, indeed, there were only twelve tablets and that she had miscounted (he kneweth how to rub things in), the wife grabbed an unmarked tablet from the pile, dug a few lines on it with her fingernail, and set it beside the previously counted tablets. Then—"

"That's *not* how the term a 'baker's dozen' came into being," blurted Lovey hotly.

"Who died and made you queen of trivia?" Peaches shot back.

Lovey narrowed her eyes. "I despise you."

Peaches smoldered. "I abominate *you*."

"I abhor you!"

"I *loathe* you!"

"Loathe *this*!"

There you have it: "Loath" (pronounced with the same "th" sound that's in "tooth") means unwilling, reluctant. "Loathe" (pronounced with the same "th" sound as in "smooth") means to hate.

Examples

➤ The Greek philosopher Diogenes was *loath* to pay rent plus utilities, so he took up residence in a tub.

➤ Filbert *loathed* riddles, such as, What has four legs and an arm?*

➤ It wasn't so much that Alexander the Great enjoyed throwing his weight around; he just *loathed* hanging around the house.

➤ *Loath* to let his nose keep him from socializing, Pinocchio hung a few doughnuts on it and went to the park.

*A pitbull

BOTTOM LINE: Scheherazade, who was married to Scharriar-the-Easily-Diverted, *loathed* storytelling, but she was much more *loath* to lose her head; and so, to keep Scharriar from killing her, she told him a story a night for 1,001 nights. (There are no details about what happened on night 1,002.)

THE GRAMMATICALLY
CORRECT HANDBOOK
THE GRAMMATICALLY
CORRECT HANDBOOK
THE GRAMMATICALLY
CORRECT HANDBOOK
THE GRAMMATICALLY
CORRECT HANDBOOK
THE GRAMMATICALLY
CORRECT HANDBOOK
THE GRAMMATICALLY
CORRECT HANDBOOK
THE GRAMMATICALLY
CORRECT HANDBOOK
THE GRAMMATICALLY
CORRECT HANDBOOK
THE GRAMMATICALLY

② Mindbenders

(Gulp)

Prophecy, Philosophy—But, Philosophize, Prophesy

Madame Celeste let her eyes roll back into her head and grasped Lila's hand. "You have suffered great sorrow of late."

Lila, whose eyes were puffy, sniffled.

"Someone close to you has hurt you terribly."

"Yeah! I'll say he did."

"A sweetheart."

Lila put her hand to her mouth.

Madame Celeste opened one eye and regarded Lila. "His name is"—she spotted the small tattoo on Lila's knee—"*Fred*."

Shocked, Lila gaped at Madame Celeste. At that moment, the fax machine became active. Madame Celeste came out of her trance and retrieved the message. "Oh, my dear!" She squeezed Lila's hand. "You have been chosen by my spirit guide to be a 'receiver'!"

Lila's eyes widened. "Yeah?"

"For a slightly larger donation, only seventy-five dollars, my guide will pass on to you knowledge from his *own* master guide."

Lila's eyes narrowed. "Yeah? How do you get the money to him?"

"Oh, my child, like me, my spirit guide is nonmaterialistic. The donation goes to Strengthen Spirituality Worldwide, an organization whose *philosophy* is to achieve world peace by making all societies on the planet aware of their spiritual side. And, as you well might guess, it takes resources to *philosophize* in a number of foreign tongues."

"But what about Fred and I?"* Lila said apprehensively.

Madame Celeste laughed fondly. "I will *of course* continue to *prophesy* your relationship with Fred. Only"—she eyed Lila—"with a more finely tuned concentration, since my concern for humanity will be considerably abated."

Lila seemed confused.

Madame Celeste smiled. "My *prophecies* about your future together will be ongoing—I *assure* you."

And Lila took out her Visa card.

There are no such words as "prophesize, prophesizing, prophesized." (No, I don't know why.) The following words, however, do exist:

Prophecy (pra-feh-see)—a prediction: Who'll win the Oscar for Best Actor?

Prophesy (pra-feh-sigh)—to predict: Steven Seagal won't. Come on, Steven Seagal?

Prophecies (pra-feh-sees)—predictions: Which couples featured on *Hard Copy* on July 4 will still be entwined by Halloween?

---

*Lila's a lost cause. You can tell her it's "about Fred and me" until the cows come home, and she'll still muck it up.

Prophesied (pra-feh-sighed)—having predicted: Aaron would move back in with Aunt Jess after graduating from law school.

> **POINTED TIP:** You already know it's "philosophy, philosophize, and philosophized."
>
> Remember that "prophecy" and "prophecies" are spelled with a "c," and the last syllable is pronounced "see(s)." "Prophesy" and "prophesied" are spelled with an "s," and the last syllable is pronounced "sigh(ed)."

Aunt Sylvie's prophecy about their vacation on the shore proved to be prophetic. "You prophe*sied* correctly," sighed Uncle Sy. "Get me some ice for my sunburned thighs."

Very **Q**uick **Q**uiz

Circle the correct choice(s) in each of the following:

1. Madame Celeste's spirit guide, Mi Sha Goss, (prophesized/prophesied) that Lila could be relied upon to keep them on Easy Street for some time. Madame Celeste's spirit guide had a knack for those kinds of (prophecies/prophesies).
2. Mi Sha Goss came from an ancient Indo-European people, the Yen Taws, who spent at least one day a week (philosophizing/philosophying) about the meaning of the king's inability to snap his fingers along with the music.
3. "I'm telling you guys," Cassandra said, "if you wheel in that big wooden horse the Greeks left outside, you're really asking for it." But the Trojans didn't believe she had the gift of (prophecy/prophesy) and could (prophesize/prophesy) the future, so they opened the gate and got what they were asking for.

Answers

❶ prophesied, prophecies (What did I just tell you? There is no such word as *prophesized*! And the "s" goes in the other one.)

❷ philosophizing (The king also sang out of tune and was a pain to have around during community sings.)

❸ prophecy, prophesy (No one believed Tiny Tim, either, when he said that someday he'd be big and strong enough to sing on the *Ed Sullivan Show*.)

BOTTOM LINE: "There is no rhyme or reason," said Hy, "you prophesy(sigh), and prophesied (sighed)"; while, on the very same day, said Kai, who was equally wise, "It's philosophy(fee) and philosophize(fize)."

There Is?

There Are?

Now, hear me well, both near and far:
Whenever "there is" more than one,
You *must* call on "There are!"

As in:

- ➤ There is a dead fly on your collar.
- ➤ There are greasy smudges on your elbow patches.
- ➤ There is an ingrown hair on your chin.
- ➤ There are a dozen other reasons you won't make the cover of *GQ* this year.

But, notice this:

➤ There *is a range* of escape routes, if the entertainment sucks.
➤ There *are a number* of reasons to pack a rod when visiting my cousin Minnie.
➤ There *are a variety* of hot sauces to choose from, including one that sears the entire digestive tract.
➤ There *is the number* of pratfalls to consider before engaging Chevy Chase.
➤ There *is the odd variety* of vampire—quite thin—that feeds on honest Hollywood agents.

"A variety" and "a number" indicate "several, more than one." "The variety" and "the number" indicate "just one."

Quick Quiz

Circle the correct choice(s) in each of the following:

1. "(There is/There are) the theory that Dr. Mower was devoured by a water buffalo; you know, the beast that seems to comb its horns in a flip," said Asquith, sipping his juice.
2. Whenever Canute shows his slides, (there is/there are) a good deal of cackling in the audience.
3. (There is/There are) nothing to be gained by abstaining from Audra's dumplings, although (there is/there are) lots of benefits to be had from imbibing her tea.
4. Ferris Wheel always performed at his best when (there were/there was) a crowd watching.
5. (There was/There were) an assortment of 8-by-10-inch glossies of Vincent Price in the box under Helmut's saws.
6. On our seven-day cruise, (there is/there are) much to do. (There is/There are) pantomime parades, marathon recitals, and quick-draw matches.

7. (There is/There are) something petty, irritating, and offensive about cutting in line at the ladies' room.

8. As Weldon said before he dropped a stitch, "(There is/There are) going to be questions about this yarn in years to come, if I have anything to say about it."

9. Come May, (there is/there are) fruit and Frisbees in the glen.

10. "In the old days," said Bryce, "(there was/there were) Fenwick and the king to kick around. Now, (there is/there are) no one worth a good boot."

Answers

❶ **there is** (Asquith's "juice" was 100 percent proof.)

❷ **there is** (In Canute's circle, cackling signifies acute boredom, and gunshots signify the end of the lecturer.)

❸ **there is, there are** (Either way, Audra expects a tip.)

❹ **there was** (Insufferable ham.)

❺ **there was** (You got a better place for them?)

❻ **there is, there are** (Mr. Whistler, who is a sketch to begin with, usually wins the quick-draws.)

❼ **there is** (You *sure* you wanna cut in, sister? I ain't sayin' you'll get hurt, but I ain't sayin' you won't. Get it?)

❽ **there are** (Always thinking, that Weldon.)

❾ **there are** (Ah, spring!)

❿ **there were, there is** (Poor baby.)

Another way to look at it: Get rid of "there" and turn things around, to see whether you need "is/are/was/were/etc.":

1. "the theory *is* that Dr. Mower was devoured . . ."
2. "a lot of cackling *is* in the audience . . ."
3. "nothing *is* to be gained; lots of benefits *are* to be had . . ."
4. "a crowd *was* watching . . ."
5. "an assortment of glossies *was* in the box . . ."
6. "much *is* to do; shipboard hunts, pantomime parades, etc. *are* . . ." (awkward, yes, but we all can't be gazelles)

7. "something *is* petty, irritating, and offensive . . ."
8. "questions *are* going to be . . ."
9. "fruit and Frisbees *are* . . ."
10. "Fenwick and the king *were* . . .; no one . . . *is* . . ."

BOTTOM LINE: "*There are* more *things* on earth than *there is time* to investigate them, so I'm out of here," said the mouse. With a final "Hickory, dickory, dock!" he beat it, leaving the clock standing there with nothing but time on its hands.

When an "Ess" Just Won't Do

TREVOR KNUMB: Welcome to "Early News," the BBC's* monthly radio roundup of events in the world of archaeology. Today's guest is Dr. Gillian Simple, professor meretricious of the Dionysius Institute of Gdansk.

GILLIAN SIMPLE: Good to be here, Trevor.

TK: I understand your recent discovery has caused quite a stir among the *media*. Please tell us about it, Doctor.

GS: Well, four years ago, my team and I applied for a grant to research—

TK: —I'm afraid we've only got fifteen minutes, Doctor. I wonder if you could get to the bottom of things, the basic *data*, if you would.

*Bedeviled Broadcasting Company

GS (pause; then, haughtily): There were thirteen Caesars who ruled ancient Rome, not twelve.

(dead air)

TK: Could you . . . could you elaborate somewhat?

GS: You want me to elaborate? What about your precious schedule? We don't want to run over into the next program, do we? I'll tell you what, Trev—(sound of chair scraping)—*you* elaborate. (voice fading) *I* wouldn't want to bore your listeners with all the bloody details!

TK (off-mike): Get her back here, damn it!

ENGINEER: She's gone, guv.

TK: Ladies and gentlemen, we seem to have had a bit of a mix-up. Uh, let's see (sound of shuffling papers), Dr. Simple was going to tell us about poking around some very old caves in . . . (coughs) where she unearthed the very old diaries of, um, a previously unknown emperor . . . who . . . (more papers shuffling) seems to have ruled for a couple of weeks—

ENGINEER: Four minutes, Trevor.

TK: —Yes, well, his name was Caesar Insipidus. He seems to have been the rather closely inbred, illegitimate son of Calig—

ENGINEER: Trevor—

TK: —ula, with an equally rotten temper and dreadful study habits—

ENGINEER: Trev?

TK: —and eventually, he was shut away on some island . . . somewhere . . . where he kept some diaries and . . .

ENGINEER: Thirty seconds.

TK: According to Dr. Simple, who deciphered his hideous handwriting . . . oh, my! here's quite an entry; on August XXth, there was this festival for virgins and . . .

Trev will obviously be off the air before he gets to the point, which is: Poor deluded Dr. Simple blames Caesar Insipidus for putting an "a" on the ends of certain words to indicate "more than one." To wit:

medium—indicates a single medium:
radio is a medium

television is a medium
newspapers are a medium

but, put them all together, and instead of several "mediums," you have:

M - E - D - I - A

Other "a" words you should know are

➤ *phenomenon*—a striking occurrence, such as Elgarine having something good to say about your birthday gift to her.
➤ *phenomenA*—more than one striking occurrence: Elgarine liking your gift *and* your card.
➤ *datum*—one single fact: Spitting on the sidewalk stinks. (Very few living people use "datum.")
➤ *datA*—several facts: Spitting on the sidewalk is disgusting; spitting on the sidewalk spreads God knows *what*; spitting on the sidewalk deserves swift and conclusive punishment, such as beheading.
➤ *criterion*—a single, important standard: A good receptionist has pen and paper in hand *before* he or she says, "May I take a message?"
➤ *criteriA*—two or more necessary standards: A good receptionist doesn't cut you off before you finish pronouncing the name of the person you're calling; doesn't keep you standing there like a plant while he or she continues chatting on the phone with Ronnie; doesn't call you by your first name on first sight just because you happen to share female chromosomes.

Quick Quiz

Circle the correct choice(s) in each of the following:

1. As an artist, Franklin enjoyed working in several (medium/media), but his favorite (medium/media) was emery boards.

2. A photo of Abe Lincoln grinning—now that would be a (phenomenon/phenomena).
3. When Ollie proposed to Henriette, he had no idea her (criterion/criteria) for a husband included a degree in electrical engineering, a fondness for the sketchbooks of Hokusai, and a talent for finding Waldo. If you woke Henriette at four A.M., however, she'd confess her main (criterion/criteria) was a big . . .
4. The data Dr. Klemperer collected about Martin and Lewis on his trip to the Catskills (was/were) highlighted in the latest issue of *Show Biz Bible*, under the headline, "Doc Digs Done Duo."

Answers

❶ **media, medium** (Franklin had begun his career, surprise, surprise, as proprietor of the Flair for Nails Salon.)
❷ **phenomenon** (If you were married to Mary Todd, you'd have looked like a gloomy Gus, too. Her doorbell chimed, but she was never home, wink, wink.)
❸ **criteria** (I don't know who Hokusai was either.) **criterion** ("a big *heart*." Honestly. What is it with you people?)
❹ **were** (At parties, Dr. Klemperer enjoyed singing "That's Amore" and walking on his ankles.)

BOTTOM LINE: "Data," "phenomena," "criteria," and "media" are all plural. "Datum," "phenomenon," "criterion," and "medium" aren't. They are singular.

None/No One

no   one

    no   one

        no   one

            no   one

                    NONE

"None" is a scrunched-up form of "no one," like a cartoon character after it smashes into a wall.

Or you can look at it this way: NO SINGLE ONE = NOT ONE = NONE

However you look at it, since "none" means "not a single blasted one," it is a loner. Standing apart. Pining for company. Therefore, "none" goes with "is" and other single verbs like that.

➤ "*None* of the love letters I've received *is* written in crayon," crowed Lara Louise.

Some people say "none" can sometimes go with "are" and other plurals, as in:

➤ "*None* of the *Popsicles were* luminous."*
➤ "*None* of his *tattoos were glowing* in the dark."*

My teachers didn't.

Be that as it may, other guaranteed soloists are

nobody	=	not one, single body
everybody	=	every single body
everyone	=	every single one
anybody	=	any single body
someone	=	some single one
somebody	=	some single body

➤ "Nobody knows the shovels I've seen," lamented the earthworm.
➤ Everybody was eager to try Mrs. Pomeranian's puppy chow.
➤ "Everyone goes off the deep end once in a while," said the high diver.
➤ Somebody, somewhere, is singing "Mandy."
➤ Anybody who wants to do back flips in this room must have a permit.
➤ The bear will keep going over the mountain until someone shows him the tunnel.

*(See "Amount/Number.")

In Other Words

Everybody has/does/knows
Anybody is/sees/goes
Everyone hears/flits/shows
Someone tells/feeds/mows
Nobody was/flies/blows
Somebody says/needs/throws

BOTTOM LINE: *None* means "no one"; *everybody* means "every body"; *anybody* means "any body"; *nobody* means "no body"; *everyone* means "every one"; *somebody* means "some body"; *someone* means "some one." There is just *one* in each of them (no matter what some say about "none").

She's/He's

It's/Its

There's/Theirs

Chickadee was late.
On the branch of a beech tree in Central Park, Wren sat chattering with annoyance.

Finch resettled himself. "My dear boy, calm down. She'll be here."

"You're always defending her."

Finch gave a weary whistle. "Why can't you understand how traumatic a broken heart can be?"

"Nobody told her to take up with a tern! Everyone knows those seabirds are worse than sailors. Besides, *it's* been a whole month."

"*Theirs* was a deep and consuming love," Finch declared, as Chickadee fluttered onto a nearby twig, sending a soft spray of snow into the air.

"Sorry," she chirped breathlessly.

"*She's* always sorry," rattled Wren.

"Never mind," Finch cheeped. "Now that we're all together, how shall we proceed? Shall we visit Bamboo Blinds? *Its* repasts are usually quite tasty."

"Not today, if you don't mind," said Wren. He cleared his throat, with some embarrassment. "My gizzard is off. I need a bland diet for a day or two."

Chickadee regarded him sympathetically. "I'm so sorry *he's* not well, Finch."

"Yes," Finch warbled agreeably. He studied Wren, who found it impossible to meet Chickadee's eye but managed to rasp, "*It's* nothing, really. *There's* this new strain of flu going around."

Chickadee hopped onto Wren's branch. "If you like, Wren, I could forage for some orange rind for you. *Its* content of vitamin C is supposed to be high. At least, that's what I hear."

Wren cocked his head and glanced at Chickadee. "Gee, that would be swell." He ruffled his feathers. "How about we get a jump on the others and breakfast at Chintzy Drapes? *Its feeder is so damn popular, it's* worse than the Plaza's birdbath in June!"

Together, Wren and Chickadee flew off.

Finch gave them a second's head start. Then, as he lifted into the sky toward Park Avenue, he trilled, "Lucky for Wren Chickadee lost her tern!"

Ah, that little ' (apostrophe). It has the power to cloud men's minds, so that they cannot see it. No. That's *The Shadow.* The apostrophe works like this:

There's is short for:	"there is," and, even though books don't admit this, also short for: "there has" (as in "there's been," etc.).
It's is short for:	"it is" and "it has" (as in "it's gone," etc.).
He's is short for:	"he is" or "he has" (as in "he's seen," etc.).

She's is short for: "she is" or "she has" (as in "she's known," etc.).

A N D

➤ "That's" = "*That is* none of your beeswax," said Ramona, grabbing the honeycomb. Or, "Yes! That's the jingle *that has* been driving me to distraction," explained the ferryman.

➤ "What's" = "*What is* with that flying buttress, bub?" Or, "*What has* been nesting in your belfry this week?"

➤ "How's" = "*How is* the air up there, Shaquille? ha ha!" Or, "*How has* Fido been doing since he lost custody of the yard?"

➤ "Someone's" = "*Someone is* using chlorine bleach again." Or, "*Someone has* been trying to beam down all afternoon." Or, to show ownership, "*Someone's* glove is in my soup."

➤ "Jeb's" = "*Jeb is* not much of a dirt-bike rider." Or, "*Jeb has* always preferred *Wheel of Fortune*." *Or*, to show ownership, "*Jeb's* greatest desire is to maintain a heartbeat."

➤ "Magnolia's" = "*Magnolia is* fond of mahogany." Or, "*Magnolia has* run out of furniture polish." *Or*, again with the ownership, "Where is *Magnolia's* ammonia? The windows are dirty."

➤ "TV's" = "The *TV is* watching what I'm doing." Or, "The *TV has* gone too far this time; call the cops." *Or*, to show possession, "The *TV's* signal is much improved since you turned on the set."

➤ "Everybody's" = "*Everybody is* furious with Tipper and her harp." *Or*, "*Everybody has* had it with Tipper and the strings she pulls." *Or*, to show you-know-what, "*Everybody's pedals* need to be pushed every now and then, but *Tipper's feet* weigh a ton."

Put IN *'s* when you're leaving OUT "is" or "has" following:

it

there

he

she

Do the same with:

that

what

how

someone

Jeb

Magnolia

the TV

everybody, nobody, somebody

POINTED TIP: When showing ownership of the following, you must ALWAYS say:
>   yours (no ')
>   ours (no ')
>   hers (no ')
>   theirs (no ')
>   its (no ')

POINTED TIP TWO: When you want to indicate ownership with something that ends in *s*—scissors, sneakers, or pants—or with more than one thing — bricks, hand grenades, carnivals —you can take that ' and stick it right after the *s*.
For example:

➤ The *scissors'* bluntness made it difficult for Imelda to create ransom notes.

➤ "If your *sneakers'* treads are unsound, so, too, must be your step," said the swami.

➤ Alger's *pants'* creases were on the diagonal, so he appeared to be walking into himself.

➤ "I don't know what the *bricks'* color has to do with how heavy they are," said Nyquist.

➤ When the hand *grenades'* pins went flying, the crowd took off, too.

➤ "Our *carnivals'* games are always on the up and up!" hollered the owners.

Quick Quiz

Circle the correct choice(s) in each of the following:

1. Double dollops of custard make (there's/theirs) the most luscious napoleons in town.
2. The (Parker's/Parkers') den was filled with old carburetors.
3. "(Someone's/Someones) been sleeping in my bed," said the Hollywood producer.
4. "(It's/Its) been such fun surveying that colony of mosquitoes," Carlotta told her nature group as she hurried off scratching herself. "(It's/Its) dance patterns are an inspiration!"
5. "It looks as if (there's/theirs) been an intruder in here," said the window washer, observing the bedroom. "Not at all," said Felix. "My roommate has a unique housekeeping policy. (It's/its) basic principle is push-and-shove-into-an-already-overcrowded-drawer-or-let-it-lie-where-it-falls."
6. All the (quintuplet's/quintuplets') ability to work a slide rule was nothing to write home about.
7. "(There's/Theirs) no explanation for Kelsey's behavior, but I wouldn't worry too much," the doctor said. "(It's/Its) not as if he's been running around totally naked."

8. "All right, (its/it's) not my slipper; (its/it's) (hers/her's)," admitted the stepsister.
9. If you can keep your head when others are losing (there's/theirs), what do you want, a medal?
10. This little computer went into the market because of (it's/its) fine feel for figures.

Answers

❶ theirs (God forbid they should offer a person any.)
❷ Parkers' (They didn't entertain very often.)
❸ someone's ("Tell me about it," said his ex-wife.)
❹ It's, Its (Carlotta did the lambada all the way to the drugstore.)
❺ there's, its (Go clean out a closet!)
❻ quintuplets' (But nobody modeled gloves like those gals.)
❼ There's, It's (Kelsey swore by pearls.)
❽ it's, it's, hers (If the shoe fits, fine; otherwise, can it.)
❾ theirs (And I'm sick of hearing about your bowling scores, too!)
❿ its (The other little PC ran terrifically, until I got it home.)

BOTTOM LINE:
One *slug's* gooey stuff is better than a few *slugs'* gooey stuff.
There's almost no room at the Smithsonian.
It's not *hers*, *his*, *theirs*, *ours*, or *yours*, so get lost.
Everybody's got his or her own favorite pot.
Its tail curled up on rainy days.
"*What's* new?" isn't funny to antique dealers.
Nobody's seen the *kitten's* mittens or his fedora.

You can also do this kind of thing with a great number of other words, including *why*, as in: "*Why's* everybody always picking on me?" complained the lock.

Between "You and" Who Else?

I fear that there will never be,
A time when I will hear with glee,
A man proclaim,
Sans hint of shame,
"Champagne, my dear, for you and I!"

Of course, if he said, "for you and *me*," he and I could consider a future together. And during a lull in the relationship, if he were to say, "Let's create a family tree for you, me, and the others," it would look like this:

I/me

we/us

```
they/them
you/you
            she/her
he/him
```

All right, so it doesn't look like a tree. The relationships still stand, no matter how they look. And don't tell me they look ridiculous. I'll tell you what's ridiculous: People who think they sound elegant when they say, "*between he and I.*" They don't. They sound like Nadine, the diva who sounds like rush hour traffic on her high notes.

"Me, us, her, him, them" *always* fill in the gap:

"between you and [the gap]."

"You," as you know, can go anywhere it likes, front or back.

Cut out this square and tape it to your bathroom mirror. Better you should study these relationships while you brush than ponder this: Since your image in the mirror is reversed, you can never truly see yourself from the outside, the way you really are (and you thought I wasn't deep):

between you and me
between you and us
between you and him
between you and her
between her and me
between her and them
between her and him
between him and me
between him and them
between them and me
between you and them

Now do, "She sold seashells by the seashore."

Quick Quiz

Circle the correct choice(s) in each of the following:

1. "Just between you and (I/me)," Rhoda confided, "I thought the crossword clue was 'without slacks.' I didn't realize it was 'without slack.' "

2. When it came to opting for Michael Jackson or Julia Roberts as an overnight guest, Perry had no trouble deciding between (he/him) and (she/her).*

3. Sherry was so wild about the Florida Marlins, you couldn't slip a sheet of paper between (she/her) and (they/them).*

4. "Do you mean to stand there and tell me I don't stand a chance against those Native Americans?" Custer exclaimed, eyes ablaze. "Well, Sergeant, let me tell you the difference between (I/me) and (they/them) . . ." he began, but—ppfft!—gurgle, gurgle—and the bugler played taps.

5. "Sit down, Goneril," said King Lear. "I've narrowed my heirs down to you and (she/her)." He pointed to Regan, who was stroking the wall safe.

6. Casanova squared his shoulders. "Shut up, Sophia! There's no point calling Gina names. You're put out because this thing between (she/her) and (I/me) goes way deeper than anything you and I ever had going."

7. The assemblyman has a well-defined sense of loyalty. When it comes to voting on behalf of his constituents or in the interest of Izzie Four Fingers, he has no trouble deciding between (they/them) and (he/him).*

8. In a moment of pique, Bo Peep cried, "Once and for all, stop dancing with those animals! I want to hear that it's over between you and (they/them)." But the Boy Who Cried Wolf merely smirked.

*In these sentences, can you say "between them" instead of between "him and them," "him and her," etc.? Of course, but not in this exercise.

9. Tweedle Dee sighed. "Some nights, Ethel, I swear I can't tell the difference between (he/him) and (I/me)."

10. King Arthur gave Guinevere the elbow. "This weekend trip with Lancelot is just to check out some lakeside property, am I right? There's nothing between you and (he/him), is there?"

Answers

❶ **you and me** (Consequently, Rhoda wrote "nude," instead of "taut.")

❷ **him and her*** (And the winner was . . .)

❸ **her and them*** (Oh, it's all right for *men* to be obsessed with sports!)

❹ **me and them** (Talk about a schmuck-a-roo.)

❺ **you and her** (Happy Father's Day.)

❻ **her and me** (Casanova was really sewer scum, but his public relations rep did a terrific job of keeping that out of the papers.)

❼ **them and him*** (The assemblyman likes his nose where it is and being able to cut his own meat.)

❽ **you and them** (This is how wars start. The Boy *wasn't* smirking; he'd just accidentally bitten his cheek.)

❾ **him and me** (Dum de dum dum!)

❿ **you and him** (Sure. Sure. Have another cup of mead, Your Highness.)

POINTED TIP ONE: This also applies to the following words: *for, concerning, about, to, from, regarding, with,* and a whole list of others I don't have room for. Treat them just the same as "between." I won't abide favoritism.

POINTED TIP TWO: Don't substitute "myself" for "me." "Myself" doesn't work like that. It's used for emphasis, to drive home a point, as in:

*See footnote on p. 118.

➤ "I myself would never serve fondue in this day and age," said Beatrice. "But, then, I'm *trés moderne*."

➤ "Aawwwwh, look what the baby did, all by himself!"

➤ "You yourself know what a pig Meredith is. You want to eat ribs with a slob, suit yourself."

Don't let "me" intimidate you. "Me" is a fine, upstanding word (they never did prove that "insider trading" charge).

Keep in mind that "me" is what you want when you say things such as: "Astrid had Kirk and *me* in stitches." From now until kingdom come, you can *never* say: "Astrid had Kirk and I in stitches."

After all, if only you and Astrid were present, while she recounted her escapades in St. Paul, would you later say: "Astrid had *I* in stitches"?

Not while I'm alive and kicking.

Linwood, how would you recount the time the sheriff invited you to vacate the premises?

"Um, he told me to beat it?"

Right. Suppose you were with Naomi and the campers at the time?

"He told Naomi, the campers, and me to beat it?"

Give that boy some Raisinets!

BOTTOM LINE: In a sentence, "you," "I," "he," "she," "we," and "they" always appear first. Their relatives, "you," "me," "him," "her," "us," and "them," show up later (if invited).

He Played

Aggressive . . .

"This is Ike Ensdorf with the postgame report. I'm in the Elks' locker room with No-Knees Nagansky, who played *brilliant*. Tell me about that interception in the second quarter. You did it just *beautiful*."

"Well, I knew if I played *aggressive*, I could get my hands on the ball."

"Thanks, No-Knees. Now, on to Salli Rae with the latest in women's gymnastics."

"Thanks, Ike. I'm here with eight-year-old Lara Landry, the new Junior Miss Gymnastics Champion. You did just *terrific*, Lara. How does it feel to be champ?"

(giggle, giggle)

"On the floor exercise, you did that last tumbling pass *real easy*. What were you thinking?"

(shrugs)

"Congratulations, Lara. Now back to the . . . uh, actually I'm told we'll be hearing from Roddy with a report on spring training."

"Thanks, Salli Rae. With me is the veteran Doves' broadcaster, Zeke Robustelli. How does the team look to you so far, Zeke?"

"I think we're in for a *real* good year. Dunwoody is pitching *outstanding*. He's painting the corners *beautiful*. If the fielding holds up, we could see a championship this year."

"Thanks, Zeke. Now, back to Penny in the studio."

Listen up. If you want to make it in the brutal arena of sports or sports broadcasting, you'll have to give up family life, sleep, and "ly."

If you want to do something else in life, however, "ly" is a must at the end of certain words, in certain instances.

Examples

➤ Jack Benimble vaulted *gracefully* over the candlestick.

➤ Mr. Wilson eyed the doctor *skeptically* when he said, "Your wife, Mary, had a little lamb."

➤ Daisy groaned *regretfully*. "Oh, no. I'm going to miss the Friends of Fickus meeting next Friday."

➤ "Is he bringing that big ox to dinner?" asked Mrs. Sprat. She wasn't speaking *rudely;* Paul Bunyan was coming over, and Mrs. Sprat was alluding to Babe.

➤ John Henry did a *really* fine job showing up that steam drill with his own two hands.

Usually, you stick "ly" on the ends of words that answer the question "How?" regarding something or someone. You must ask that question yourself. Don't expect anyone else to do it for you.

Take the examples above:

➤ *How* did Jack Benimble vault over the candlestick? Gracefully (just as his mother taught him).

➤ *How* did Mr. Wilson eye the doctor? Skeptically (Mr. Wilson trusted his wife).

➤ *How* did Daisy groan? Regretfully (she was looking forward to seeing her friend, Fhyllis).

➤ *How* did Mrs. Sprat speak? Not rudely (she made catty remarks about Babe *after* they left).

➤ *How* fine a job did John Henry do? Really (only thing is, then he dropped dead).

If we apply this "how" rule to the broadcasters' reports, they would read as follows:

"This is Ike Ensdorf with the postgame report. I'm in the Elks' locker room with No-Knees Nagansky, who played *brilliantly*. Tell me about that interception in the second quarter. I know there isn't much to say—an interception is an interception, but you did it *beautifully*. Can you give us a few words?"

"Well, I knew if I became aggressive and elbowed Hatcher *viciously*, I could get my hands on the ball."

"Thanks, No-Knees. Now, on to Salli Rae with the latest in women's gymnastics."

"Thanks, Ike. I'm here with eight-year-old Lara Landry, the new Junior Miss Gymnastics Champion. Lara, how does it feel to be champ?"

(Lara looks at her mother, who whispers to her.) Lara says, "It's *veritably* a thrill."

"On the floor exercise, you did that last tumbling pass *really easily*. What were you thinking?"

(Lara looks at her mother, who whispers to her.) Lara says, "All those hours practicing, while my coach screamed bloody murder, paid off *handsomely*."

"Congratulations, Lara. Now back to the . . . uh, actually I'm told we'll be hearing from Roddy with a report on spring training."

"Thanks, Salli Rae. With me is the Doves' veteran broadcaster, Zeke Robustelli. How does the team look to you so far, Zeke?"

"I think we'll be playing *successfully* this year. Dunwoody is pitching *outstandingly*. He's painting the corners *beautifully*. *Confidentially*, though, if he starts boozing again, there goes the whole ball game."

"Thanks, Zeke. Now back to Penny in the studio."

Quick Quiz

Circle the correct choice(s) in each of the following:

1. "Every now and then, I feel (uncontrollable/uncontrollably) tempted to mow the Sheep Meadow in Central Park," said Mah Jong (sheepish/sheepishly).

2. You'd have thought Oedipus' mother would have (definite/definitely) recognized him from the birthmark on his behind before she married him.

3. The Montgolfier brothers did not behave (courageous/courageously) in Paris in 1783, when the manned balloon they invented lifted off for the first time. They weren't the (heroic/heroically) guys sitting (valiant/valiantly) in the basket.

4. With one hole to play on the back nine, Galen (flagrant/flagrantly) broke the rules by shouting, "There's a UFO!" and then tossing the ball into the cup.

5. "Maximus says the gladiators are fighting too (sluggish/sluggishly)," said the manager of the Coliseum. The captain of the guards replied, "*You* go tell those apes not to frolic so (exuberant/exuberantly) after hours."

6. Clayton began hitting backhands more (smooth/smoothly) once he put on larger shorts.

7. In the 200-meter backstroke, Antonia kicked so (wild/wildly), she banged into the wall of the pool and knocked herself out.

8. "Oh, my God!" said Mr. Hemingway (fearful/fearfully). "It's a hooded pitohui!"

9. No matter how (tight/tightly) Lisa Marie corkscrewed herself, she couldn't pull off a triple lutz.

10. Hamilton and Hana came in last in the ice dancing competition because she began snorting (hysterical/hysterically) during their "Hootie and the Blowfish" sequence.

Answers

❶ **uncontrollably, sheepishly** (Mah Jong shared this revelation on the first episode of *I Confess*, coming soon to your local station.)

❷ **definitely** (Mother Oedipus *must* have seen him working out in the gym, and in those days, the only thing those guys wore was olive oil.)

❸ **courageously, heroic, valiantly** (Would *you* have gone up in a balloon if you could have found two meatba—, uh, two daredevils to go instead?)

❹ **flagrantly** (Galen's golf buddies weren't fooled for a minute. But since they had him this close to investing in a groundbreaking burger chain in India, they kept quiet.)

❺ **sluggishly, exuberantly** (In the end, the manager jotted down Maximus's suggestion and had a slave run it over to the gladiators' quarters.)

❻ **smoothly** (I have nothing to add.)

❼ **wildly** (And guess who still came in third?)

❽ **fearfully** (Awwwww. Big, brave man when it comes to killing rhinos and elephants, but one little poisonous bird shows up and Mr. Hemingway turns into a big wuss!)

❾ **tightly** (Finally, she took up with Hamilton. See below.)

❿ **hysterically** (Hamilton ditched Hana when she begged him to add Velcro to their costumes, for a "seamless look" on the ice. He and Lisa Marie are debuting a fitness video called *Skating to Thin on Ice*!)

BOTTOM LINE: Give me an "l"! Give me a "y"! Put 'em together at the end of a word to describe:

- ➤ *how* Maid Marian treated Robin Hood (seductively)
- ➤ *how* U. S. Grant drank (lip-smackingly)
- ➤ *how* Amelia Earhart flew (disastrously, that last time)
- ➤ *how* Sir Walter Raleigh behaved when he threw his cape over that puddle so that Queen Elizabeth I could cross the street (cavalierly, or like a yutz, depending on whose corner you're in).

A Word or Two for Less of "More"

"The Case of the Addled Hungarian"

Miss Marmalade put down her pen and squinted at her watch. Menacing clouds, *darker* than the ash in her fireplace, had gathered outside her windows (which were the *grimiest* in Smoked-salmonshire*), and her library was *dimmer* now than it had been this morning when she had begun her accounts, which were *harder* to settle now that she was investing in pork futures.

Miss Marmalade's watch said half-past. It was late, *later* than she'd thought, but not the *latest* it had ever been, at this time of

*Pronounced "Lox."

day. Still, besides finishing her correspondence before tea, Miss Marmalade had planned to cycle into Mushroom-on-Barley to call on the vicar, who'd been sneezing. What a pity! This autumn had been his *hardiest* in years.

There was a soft rapping at the library door. "Come," Miss Marmalade called, in a voice *brighter* and *livelier* than her spirits, but not *deeper* than the furrows on her brow. "Sorry to disturb you, mum." Frail Mrs. Grimsby tottered into the room. A phlegmatic woman, she was *older*, *slower*, and *shorter* than the other servants Miss Marmalade had employed, but by far the *dearest*—and *cheapest*—(if the *rockiest*) of the lot. "Inspector McFamischt would like a word with you, mum."

"Oh, my," Miss Marmalade responded, "I hope there hasn't been another murder. I've so very much to do today. Moreover, I've yet to be imbursed by the constabulary for solving the last case, which was the *trickiest* puzzle I've encountered so far. As you'll recall, Mrs. Grimsby, it involved a dying earl of great wealth and an incalculable number of greedy relatives, each so much *greedier* than the next that it was impossible to designate the *greediest*."

Eyes half-closed, Mrs. Grimsby tottered. Miss Marmalade was about to remonstrate with her for not keeping both feet on the ground when the door flew open. Inspector McFamischt hurried into the room. Perceptively, Miss Marmalade noted that he was not alone. Beside him wavered a young, bewildered man, who she immediately determined was not English. He was wearing loud colors and chattering in a foreign tongue, *stranger* to Miss Marmalade's ear than even American English.

"Miss Marmalade," began the inspector, but at that moment a shot rang out.

"Paprikash!" cried the young man, and he fell to the floor.

"I believe," Miss Marmalade announced, with *sharper* acumen and *greater* poise than might be expected at such a moment, "I believe he is Hungarian. And, I might add," she added, in her *surest* tone, "*deader* than a doornail."

Where has "-er" gone?

➤ Tasha is *plainer* than Masha.
➤ Janna is *vainer* than Lana.
➤ Cedric is *gamer* than Friedrich.

And what of "-est"?

➤ Meredith has the *poshest* cottage in Monaco.
➤ Unfortunately, she also has the *dreariest* personality.
➤ Nevertheless, her current beau is the *handsomest* bum playing volleyball on the beach.

More and more these days, "more" is moving in on "-er." *More* smug. *More* bulky. *More* eerie. Why? Did some piece of e-mail go out warning people off "-er"? Listen: "-er" is nonfattening, non-polluting, and the price is right: It doesn't cost any more than "more." All I ask, then, is that you give "-er" a chance.

Look, even if I wanted you to consign "more" to the Hall of Words Past Their Prime, along with "Yo, Adrienne!" and "affordable housing," you can't. You have to say things such as "more intricate" and "most desirable." "Intricater" and "desirablest" are strictly for them what don't know the rules.

Sad to say, I have no foolproof rule for when to use "more" to emphasize the word following it. If your ear doesn't tell you that "pitifuller" is wrong, open the dictionary. I'm confident you will discover whether the word in question can take -er, -ier, -est, or -iest without dying of shame.

Examples

➤ You can cook flan that's *more savory* than Pru's, and *tastier* than Hortense's.
➤ Your skis may be in a *more pitiful* state than Cyril's, but Hedy's may be the *sorriest*.
➤ Your mental outlook may be *more harmonious* than Dudley's, but the Buddhist monk's down the block may be the *serenest*.

➤ Your screams during parachuting class may be *noisier* than Bart's, but his may be *more earsplitting*.

➤ Your assessment of Chelsea's mastery of the tambourine may be *more knowledgeable* than Stella's, yet Pia's may be *nicer* (as in "precise").

➤ You may consider lawyers *more scurrilous* than restaurant workers who prepare food without a hairnet, but Lucas may consider financial consultants *lousier*.

➤ You may prefer a *more unadorned*, beaded headband, while Nathaniel Hawthorne may insist upon an even *simpler* ornament.

➤ You may consider Eloise *more snobbish* than the count, but the countess may be the *snottiest* of all.

➤ You may think Myrtle was *more uninhibited* than Mary Ellen at the blackjack table and that Graham was *drunker* at the slot machines.

➤ You may hope that Luther will be *more indulgent* of your two-step and LouAnn *kinder* when it comes to your spelling.

➤ You may be *more frightened* of bats than roaches but find that guy down the hall who keeps a hooded vulture in the foyer *creepier*.

BOTTOM LINE: Let me be clearer, more forthcoming. Don't just think about using "-er" and saving "more" for special occasions—*do it!* An "-er" (or "-ier") in the right place can do just as much, if not more, than the maddening, repetitive use of "more." The same goes for an "-est" (or "-iest") at the end of a word to express "most." You can point out that "Wonder Woman is *spryer* than Cat Woman and vaults the *highest* Andes without breaking into a sweat, much less breathing hard. Nyah nyah nyah."

To "Wh**o**/Wh**o**m"

It Sh**ou**ld

C**o**ncern

Who? Whom? Who? Whom?
It's enough to make your nerves race.
Whom? Who? Whom? Who?
Hey, all you need know is "about-face!"

Actually, you need to know one thing more:

"Who" stands for "he" or "she."
"Whom" is a substitute for "him" or "her."

All together:

he/she/who
him/her/whom

This is where the "about-face" comes in. Anytime you don't know whether to use "who" or "whom," turn the words around to see whether you'd substitute "he/she" or "him/her." For instance:

➤ Edna May's boyfriend, (who/whom) she describes as a "neurotic scumbag," *is*.

Now, if you take "(who/whom) she describes" and turn it around, you get "she describes (who/whom)." Would you say, "she describes 'he' "? or "she describes 'him' "? (Hint: HIM HIM HIM HIM HIM HIM.) That's right, "she describes 'him.' " And what can we substitute for "him"? (Hint: WHOM WHOM WHOM WHOM WHOM.)

Hot dog. The way to go is

➤ Edna May's boyfriend, *whom* she describes as a "neurotic scumbag," is too well-adjusted for her anyway.

POINTED TIP: The same goes for "whoever" ("he-she"ever) and "whomever" ("him-her"ever).

POINTED TIP TWO: If you don't know whether to use "who" or "whom" in a situation where it doesn't make sense to do an about-face, substitute "he/she-him/her" to see which works:

➤ The female woodchuck (who/whom) chucks the most wood would chuck it all for a desk job.

Would you say "she chucks" or "her chucks"? (Psst: SHE SHE SHE SHE SHE.)
Therefore, you would say:

➤ The female woodchuck *who* chucked the most wood didn't get the promotion.

Quick Quiz

Circle the correct choice(s) in each of the following:

1. "I'm lookin' for Myrtle Beach," rasped the thug, "(who/whom) I figure has stolen the goods Van Couver told her to stash."
2. "(Who/Whom) shall I say is calling?" Jeannette asked Nelson.
3. The art dealer (who/whom) sold fake Vermeers was a regular at Neighborhood Crime Watch meetings.
4. "I adore (whoever/whomever) adores me," admitted Lolly.
5. The inexperienced llama rancher, (who/whom) everyone said needed to have his head examined, made millions and bought a country.
6. Glen Cove renounced his dance teacher, (who/whom) he'd seen shredding a photo of Fred Astaire.
7. "One Mississippi, two Mississippi, three . . ." counted Carmichael, (who/whom) Austin had dubbed "it."
8. The pastry chef (who/whom) always had a bun in the oven often missed work.
9. Raising his baton, the conductor whispered to the percussionists, "I'm depending on (whoever/whomever) is playing the triangle for a righteous 'ding.' "
10. Zinnia had not heard from Gareth, (who/whom) she had last seen in the Fun House at Coney Island.

Answers

❶ **who** "I figure (she) has stashed . . ." (The wind didn't blow between Myrtle's ears.)

❷ **who** "I should say (he/she) is calling . . ." (When I'm calling youuuuuuu, pick up the phone!)

❸ **who** "(he/she) sold fake Vermeers . . ." (The art dealer was also on the board of several HMOs.)

④ whoever "(he-who) adores me." (Lolly liked crunchy and smooth peanut butter, chocolate and vanilla, closed- and open-toed shoes, fat men and thin; in short, she had no taste.)

⑤ who "everyone said (he) needed his head examined . . ." (He did. The rancher had an irrational fear of pumice stones.)

⑥ whom "he'd seen (him) shredding . . ." (What was Glen Cove supposed to do, go back to perfecting his fox trot as if nothing had happened?)

⑦ whom "Austin had dubbed (him) . . ." (While Carmichael stood there counting, naughty Austin lit out for the Baltic.)

⑧ who "(she) always had a bun in the oven . . ." (The pastry chef spent much too much time with the guy who iced her cakes.)

⑨ whoever "(he/she-who) is playing the triangle . . ." (One righteous ding is worth a heap of dongs.)

⑩ whom "she had last seen (him) . . ." (One minute he was scrutinizing himself in the skinny mirror, and the next he was a memory.)

BOTTOM LINE: who = he/she
whom = him/her

Look at it this way. Suppose you were casting a revival of *Our Town*. *Whom* would you want to play the old, cracker-barrel New England "stage manager"? Tony Danza? (Would you really want *him*?)

And *whom* would you want to play dear, sweet Emily, *who* bites the dust before she can get fed up with her husband? One of those bombshells from *Baywatch* who sashay around in bikinis all the time? Would you really want *her*?

Think about it.

Who/That/

Which/Huh?

Good evening, ladies and gentlemen, my name is Jerry Jackie, and I'm happy to be here tonight.

How'd you like the play, Mrs. Lincoln? She says, "I didn't get to see it!"

But, seriously—did you hear the one about the guy that (1) went to Rome? When he got home, his friend said, "Did you throw a coin in the fountain that (2) brings you luck?" The guy says, "No." "Why not?" says the friend. "I didn't have a coin," says the guy (two, three, four, five, six)—"so I tossed in a traveler's check!"

Say, did you hear about the inventor that (3) thought up a wonderful electric car? On just $10 worth of electricity you can go from coast to coast—twice. Oh, yeah—you need a $600,000 extension cord!

I used to play poker with my friend Al, but I stopped. Would you play poker with someone that (4) cheated all the time? Well, neither would *he*! (ba rum bum)

What's Irish and stays out all night—Paddy-o furniture!

What do you call a Filipino contortionist? A Manila folder!

So there's this guy that (5) was so stupid, he locked his keys in the car and—it took him an hour to get his family out!

"Who" comes after anyone who breathes. Did you hear the one about:

➤ Jerry, the *comic who* had terrible timing, no sense of humor, and no idea when to use "who" and "that"? *Note*: In his routine, he should have said: (1) the guy who, (3) the inventor who, (4) someone who, (5) this guy who.
➤ the *club owner who* only hired him because Jerry had knocked up the club owner's daughter?
➤ the *punk* at the bar *who* decided enough was enough and knocked Jerry into oblivion?
➤ the *lawyer who* pleaded the punk's case?
➤ the *judge who* let the punk off because he'd seen Jerry's act?

"Who" may also come after an animal you know and love (because I say so):

➤ Kipling's Rikki-Tikki-Tavi, the mongoose *who* made mincemeat out of cobras
➤ Shari Lewis's Meatball, uh, Lambchop, *who* was so cute, you could just eat her up
➤ Jack London's dog, whatsisname, *who* enjoyed running around in the wild

Things that don't breathe (and animals you're not crazy about) are followed by "that":

- *Note*: In his routine, Jerry's friend correctly said, "(2) the *fountain that*"
- the *stamp that* didn't stick
- the *bank CD that* earned zip
- Fletcher's *wit that* was far from "quip"
- the *candle that* had a wilted wick
- the *pot roast that* was so dry it made Morris sick
- the *corn plant that* grew so tall it hit the roof*

When it comes to "which," most people use it willy-nilly, all over the place. This is how I was taught to use it:

"Which" starts a thought that comes after a comma. The comma is a flashing light that indicates one of two things:

1. Hey! This thought is so important, you need to set it off by itself and take a breath beforehand, and the comma allows you to do that.
2. (Yawn) Like empty calories, this idea doesn't contribute anything. It's an afterthought, an idle something that just came to me.

Examples

- Lightning may strike twice, which is why Ben Franklin only flew his kite in the rain that one time.
- Genghis Khan didn't waste time talking things out, which didn't affect his hordes one way or the other.

Quick Quiz

Circle the correct choice(s) in each of the following:

1. An olive ridley, (that/which) sounds like something Noël Coward sipped at cocktail parties, is a big sea turtle.

*When plants *talk* as well as breathe, you can give them a "who." Until then, they get a "that."

2. "You remember Dennis. He was the guy (that/who) wore the tie (that/who) had snowmen all over it."

3. "For just $99.95 down, you can own a genuine replica of the hat (that/who) Carmen Miranda wore, the one (that/who) had bananas all over it."

4. Mrs. Feld affectionately touched Mrs. O'Hara's arm. "I love Patrick McGoohan, too! Didn't he play the man on TV (that/who) owned a fancy island?"

5. "No, Vanessa, bank voles are not the same as bank vaults. Bank voles are small animals (that/who) look like lemmings. Bank vaults are the places (that/who) Aunt Bonnie and Uncle Clyde liked to visit."

6. Eg was the first caveman (that/who) discovered you could kill time by drawing circles on the wall.

7. The Colossus of Rhodes, (which/that) was built a really long time ago, was one of the Seven Wonders of the Ancient World. It was made of bronze and was supposed to be Apollo, (who/that) was a big god at the time. The statue stood in the harbor of an island (who/that) was called Rhodes. It still is.

8. Sepek takraw is a game (that/who) is played on a badminton court in Southeast Asia.

9. George Orwell's *Animal Farm* is often called an allegory, (which/that) means Orwell was able to write on more than one level.

10. General George McClellan was the kind of military leader (that/who) liked a battle (that/who) had the other side outnumbered by about a million. During the Civil War, he made a lot of mistakes running the army of the Potomac, (which/that) may be why he was later elected governor of New Jersey.

Answers

❶ **which** (It is so!)

❷ **who, that** (You know, the guy who left with Manny's date.)

❸ **that, that** (Fresh tropical fruit in season is extra.)

❹ **who** (To: Patrick McGoohan. We all know you created and starred in *The Prisoner*, that classic TV series about a (perhaps) former government agent imprisoned on an island that wasn't a resort. On some level, even Mrs. Feld knows, but with everything she's got on her mind, now that Maurice is retiring and Dana is talking about a divorce . . . oh, forget it. And who says McGoohan'll never see this?)

❺ **that, that** (Vanessa adored Aunt Bonnie and Uncle Clyde. They sent her postcards from all over the Southwest. Her favorite showed Uncle Sam pointing his finger and saying, "I want you!")

❻ **who** (Who knows what Eg might have achieved if he'd lived past twenty-four? Andy Warhol started out with one can of soup.)

❼ **which, who, that** (The Colossus was there until the island went co-op and the board decided to put in security lights instead.)

❽ **that** (Yes, there's more than just that one badminton court.)

❾ **which** (The ground floor, the mezzanine . . .)

❿ **who, that, which** (Some of my best friends are from Jersey!)

BOTTOM LINE: The *boy who* stood on the *deck that* was burning decided to give up the sea for telemarketing, *which* was a smart move.

Let's **Agree,**

Sh**a**ll W**e**?

Elizabeth Taylor and Nicky Hilton, Jr.
Elizabeth Taylor and Michael Wilding
Elizabeth Taylor and Mike Todd
Elizabeth Taylor and Eddie Fisher
Elizabeth Taylor and Richard Burton
Elizabeth Taylor and Richard Burton
Elizabeth Taylor and John W. Warner
Elizabeth Taylor and Larry Fortensky
Bear cub and a one-room apartment

The common bond here is, sometimes things that seem to belong together—*don't*. (Bear cubs *grow*.)

When it comes to sentences, the principle is the same. For starters, a sentence is usually about something. Let's call that thing the "top." And whatever the "top" is doing (or having done to it), we'll call the "bottom." (**Jargon Alert**: Actually, the "top" is the "subject," and the "bottom" is the "predicate," or "verb and friends.") For example,

➤ Late in life, *Vincent van Gogh* (top) never *wore* (bottom) a complete pair of earrings.
➤ "Beige *espadrilles* (top) *make* (bottom) that outfit, Ceil."
➤ *Uncle Manny* (top) *plays around* (bottom).
➤ *Candied carrots* (top) *nauseate* (bottom) Leonard (who, in turn, nauseates Louise).
➤ *Tom and Ray* (top) *do* (bottom) a great impression of Regis Philbin.

Obviously, the top has to match the bottom (otherwise, you're not leaving this house!). One top (singular), one bottom (singular). Lots of tops (plural), a bottom with a lot in it (plural), like Brendan before he took up aerobics.

Lots of times, though, people get confused. Why?

Geography.

At first glance, they think the top and bottom have to be right up against each other—like Georgia and Florida—when, often, the real top is way over there, where Oregon is, and the bottom is in Vermont. (If you like, while I'm at it, I can explain quantum physics.) For instance,

1. According to a recent poll, one in ten submarine *commanders have* a hard time leaving the basement during shore leave.
2. Five to ten inches of *snow is expected* to ruin Monique's barbecue.
3. *Traffic and weather is coming* up on the half hour, here on NEWS.

Can you spell w-r-o-n-g? w-r-o-n-g? w-r-o-n-g?

1. How many submarine commanders hang around the house on shore leave? *One* out of every ten. ONE. Not all ten. If all ten got the jitters out in the open, the sentence would say that, and one of the networks would have a miniseries. ONE commander does. The other nine gallivant all over the place.

So, since the top is "one," the sentence should read:

"According to a recent poll, *one* (top) in ten submarine commanders *has* (bottom) a hard time leaving the basement during shore leave."

Remember, just because "commanders" is next to the "bottom" doesn't mean it has any influence over it (consider your puny donation to the senator's campaign alongside Palutem Petroleum's).

2. What's important about Monique's inept party-planning skills is the *amount* of snow predicted—"Five to ten *inches*" (top). If it were just going to snow, maybe leave a dusting or an inch at best, she might be able to pull it off. The right matchup reads:

"Five to ten *inches* (top) of snow *are expected* (bottom) to ruin Monique's barbecue."

3. I love this one. Tell me, is traffic the same thing as weather? No. They're separate, independent, boring—like math and televised golf.

You wouldn't say, "Carl and Evan *is* joining us for Monopoly," would you? (If you were smart, you wouldn't say they were joining you period.) Well, then, why in the world would you say "traffic and weather *is*"? ANSWER ME!

"*Traffic and weather* (top) *are coming* (bottom) up on the half hour, here on NEWS." That's how it goes.

Quick Quiz

Circle the correct choice(s) in each of the following:

1. One out of four county supervisors (knows/know) where the bodies are buried.
2. Hal, Henry, and Hal's wife, Honey, (is/are) taking an adult ed course called "Put New Zest in Your Love Life!"

3. Coming soon to prime-time TV: *Such a Gorgeous Bird!*, the story of a wisecracking parakeet and a family who (live/lives) in San Bernardino.

4. On a scale of one to ten, Chee Chee, the superintendent of the Paradise Apartments, (rank/ranks) fourteen.

5. Dr. Vigor has created a new line of high-energy, low-calorie, nutrition-packed products that (is/are) now on sale wherever party hats and card tricks (is/are) are carried. One month's supply (is/are) only $74.99.

6. Selma, along with her cousins from Hicksville, (is/are) putting money on Lucille to win the canasta tournament.

7. A handful of red-vested accountants (was/were) spotted comparing debit columns outside the convention hall.

8. Each of the leaves (turn/turns) against the tree, in the end.

Answers

❶ **knows** (Therefore, he, or she, never shows up for work but collects a salary anyhow.)

❷ **are** (Hmmm.)

❸ **live** (Come on. It's not just the bird *TV Guide* is going to be featuring on the cover.)

❹ **ranks** (Chee Chee, you funny little, sunny little Chee Chee.)

❺ **is, are, is** (The doctor's line is paying for his twenty-two-room retreat in Monaco.)

❻ **is** (*Selma's* the big enchilada; her cousins are just picante sauce.)

❼ **was** (So? Everybody's got to be somewhere.)

❽ **turns** (Each *one* of them *does*, the ingrates.)

Son of "**L**et's **A**gree . . ."

I'm as sick about this as you're going to be, but the one-for-one rule doesn't always apply.

I know how "series" *sounds*, but just because it's got an "ess" on the end doesn't mean you need an "ess-type" bottom. The same goes for "news." "Series" is; "news" is.

Depending on how you use it, though, "ethics" can go either way, along with others of its ilk, such as "politics," "mathematics," and "athletics."

➤ "Diddy, Cheatem, U. Bett's ethics (their *principles* of behavior) are a laugh a minute."

But,

➤ "Ethics is the course (a *single* body of study) the CEO of Gouge M. Good Pharmaceuticals slept through in college."

Quick Quiz

Circle the correct choice(s) in each of the following:

1. The series of lectures on "In-Line Skating for Money" (has/have) been postponed until Edna Ferrara's elbow heals.
2. Per your request, one million dollars (has/have) been transferred to your account.
3. The number of lizards in Uruguay (is/are) of interest to absolutely no one I know.
4. A growing number of broad jumpers (is/are) wearing springs in their shoes.

Answers

❶ **has** (Edna doesn't buy that "no pain, no glory" guff.)
❷ **has** (First, you should be so lucky. Second, you use "has" because "a million dollars" is one big wad, like bubble gum, only better for the teeth. Two tens, on the other hand, fit (not "fits") more easily in your wallet.)

❸ is (Once more, from the top, *the number* of lizards *is*. Not to worry. It'll come in time.)

❹ are (Um. Wait. Give me a minute. Right. Think of it this way: "the number" is vague. Could be seven, four thousand, twelve. But by "a number of broad jumpers," you mean more than one—several. It's like implying, "We know there is more than one of you scum-buckets out there."

POINTED TIP: Think of it like ticktacktoe. You can't have one *X* and two *O*s to win, or vice versa. They all have to match:

BOTTOM LINE: If the main point (top) in a sentence has more than one part, whatever the main point is doing, or having done to it (bottom), also has to reflect "more than one." You can't mix one apple with half a dozen pears. If one thing is singular, the other must be, too. "One does; two or more do," unless you're dealing with one of those "son of" words, in which case, "two does!"

Significant

Other of

"Let's Agree . . ."

Sometimes, "one" is a little devil, out to tempt you through the glittering arches of Grammar Hell. You can tell because it will be dressed sleazily, like this:

"one of those teacups that . . ."
"one of the swamps that . . ."
"one of our flag wavers who . . ."
"one of her conniptions that . . ."
"one of several sprinters who . . ."

As soon as you spot "one" in this getup,

you've

    got

        to

            toss

                that

                    "*one*"

out, with last year's *People*'s "in" list. Concentrate on:

"teacups—that . . ."
"swamps—that . . ."
"flag wavers—who . . ."
"conniptions—that . . ."
"sprinters—who . . ."

Ask yourself, What do all these *teacups and swamps and flag wavers and conniptions and sprinters do*? (You don't care what each "*one*" of them *does*; neither do I.)

Well, since you ask,

➤ It was one of *those precious, little teacups that think* they're better than Styrofoam.
➤ We came upon one of *the swamps that beg* to be side-stepped.
➤ N. Dorphin was one of *our flag wavers who like* to march in a brisk wind, wearing shorts.
➤ When Rhondee Vou has one of *her conniptions that threaten* her career as a pacifist, the city weeps.
➤ Jared was one of *several sprinters who don't sit* still for anything.

B*U*L*L*E*T*I*N

This just in. In an effort to make you look like a schlemiel, "one" is often seen in the company of "only." As in,

Orlando is the *only one of the commodores who has* a wife named Pistachio.

In this case, the emphasis is on *just one* of the commodores. If you were to say, "Orlando is one of the commodores who have a wife named Pistachio," you'd be referring to numerous commodores who have suspiciously similar tastes in women.

Quick Quiz

Circle the correct choice(s) in each of the following:

1. Skipping is one of those activities that (is/are) confined to the human animal.
2. "As far as I'm concerned, Dr. Pangloss is one of those professors who (has/have) (their/his) head(s) screwed on backward," said Candy.
3. Jack Rabbit is the only one of the guys who (fall/falls) head over heels at the sight of floppy ears.
4. I. Fultauer had one of those attitudes that (demand/demands) heads-back respect.
5. "I assure you, gentlemen, investing your time here is one of those ventures that (pay/pays) off in the long run," said the warden.
6. "I'm going to give you the only one of my questionnaires that (is/are) rigged," said the political pollster to the investigative reporter.

Answers

❶ **are** (You know any turkeys that skip?)
❷ **have, their** (heads) (Imagine Candy's chagrin after

spending a bundle on textbooks for the course that yutz taught.)

❸ **falls** (Excuse me, do *all* the guys have a thing for floppy ears, or *just* Jack? Thank you.)

❹ **demand** (Eye, full, tower . . . yawn)

❺ **pay** (To bring his point home to the "gentlemen," the warden brandished a big piece of wood with nails in it.)

❻ **is** (What a patriot.)

BOTTOM LINE: This is one of those entries that require your complete attention—so, wake up!

"They" Ain't the Only Game in Town

Nobody noticed when Arizona entered the saloon. AZ was not the kind of man you noticed, which worked in his favor.

He made his way to the bar, ordered a whiskey, took a sip, turned, and surveyed the room.

Several card games were in progress, but a raucous laugh from the table to AZ's right caught his interest. "I told you, Lem, I *told* you it was my night!" The farmer swept up the pot and gave another laugh. "When someone says they're lucky," he taunted, "you ain't supposed to mess with them!"

AZ straightened his hat and sauntered over to the table. "Evening, gentlemen. Mind if I sit in?"

"Suit yourself," said the farmer. "If you don't mind losin', I don't mind winnin'!" The other cowboys eyed AZ indifferently. Nothing distinguished him except his manicured fingernails, fancy duds, saucy mustache, exquisite boots, and crème de menthe aftershave.

The farmer dealt the cards. AZ lit a cheroot (a cigar with both ends cut, from the Tamil). He took a puff. "Tell me, gentlemen, if someone were to bet the farm, would he or she be considered courageous or crazy?"

The others were dumbfounded. "Whadya mean 'she'?" asked the farmer, warily. "Women in Valhalla don't own no farms."

AZ smiled and tossed a few pieces of silver onto the pile. "Merely a question of grammatical manners, gentlemen."

Lem shot an arc of tobacco juice in the direction of the spittoon. "Yeah, well, you better watch your gramatrickal manna, stranger—unless you're lookin' for trouble."

AZ raised his hand in a gesture of peace. "Gentlemen," he said, laying his cards faceup on the table and gathering up all the silver, "I believe it is you who had better watch your grammatical manners, unless"—he added, rising and tugging at his vest— "you are content to spend the rest of your lives in this dung pit, toiling at menial tasks."

AZ would have gone on about the value of good grammar and smelling nice, but Miss Eezie, who managed the saloon, sidled up to him. She was wearing a gown very much cinched at the waist, with a snug, deeply cut bodice, and after a moment or two, AZ elected to go upstairs with her and discuss matters of anatomy.

That pathetic farmer got in trouble on two points: First, he said, "When *someone* says *they're* lucky, you ain't supposed to mess with *them!*" He meant, "When someone says *he or she is* lucky, you ain't supposed to mess with *him or her!*"

Second, had he said the latter, AZ would have sat down at a different table (AZ was funny that way), and the farmer wouldn't have lost the mortgage money.

"They" and "them" are unacceptable when referring to one horse trader, one dipstick, one loose end. . . .

Examples

➤ If you really love somebody, you should want what's best for them, as long as it's still good for you.

➤ Each stickball team chose their own sticks.

The foregoing should read:

➤ If you really love *somebody*, you should want what's best for *him or her*. . . .

"Somebody" means "one person, male or female," not a bunch of people. To use "them" correctly in that sentence, you could say: If you really love your *ears* or those *militiamen*, you should want what's best for *them*.

➤ *Each* stickball *team* chose *its* own sticks.

"Each . . . team" means "each individual one of them," not "all teams" or "some teams" or "a few teams." And, since "team" isn't male or female, you use "its" rather than "his" or "her." Again, if you want to use "their" in that sentence, one possibility is, *All* stickball *teams* chose *their* own sticks.

Quick Quiz

Circle any mistake(s) in each of the following:

1. Everyone orders their buffalo steak with potato puffs and a small green salad.
2. "I want to be a musician when I grow up," said Anton, "because they can really play with other musicians. A writer doesn't go to another writer's house and write with he or she."
3. "Schroeder, you are the only person I know," screamed Belmontia, "who would ask a Christian Scientist what kind of medical coverage they have!"
4. A person's ears grow as he or she ages.
5. "When someone says something you don't like on the phone, that's no reason to hang up on them," sobbed the information operator.

6. The villagers became restive when they learned that the squire was cutting back his or her minnow rights.

7. If the processed cheeses are not ripe by Wednesday, their aroma will be unappetizing, and the guests may not eat their tuna melts.

8. When opportunity knocks, don't leave them standing at the door.

9. The potters were on their best behavior, and only threw his or her clay when no one else was around.

10. No one likes to have his or her sense of humor ridiculed.

Answers

❶ *Everyone* orders *his or her* buffalo steak . . . (You wouldn't order a cheeseburger with Lyonnaise potatoes, would you?)

❷ "I want to be a *musician* when I grow up," said Anton, "because *he or she* can . . . A writer doesn't . . . write with *him or her*." (Norman, this is Gore. How about joining me Thursday night for some Dover sole and plot outlines?)

❸ ". . . ask a Christian Scientist what kind of medical coverage *he or she* has!" (Mr. Tact.)

❹ correct (I was going to take a cheap shot at Prince Charles but thought better of it.)

❺ "When *someone says* . . . no reason to hang up on *him or her*." (Oh, grow up!)

❻ The *villagers* . . . cutting back *their* rights. (Aren't you glad we no longer live in a world where all the power lies in the hands of the few?)

❼ correct (Let 'em eat dip.)

❽ When *opportunity* knocks . . . leave *it* . . . (Only FedEx knocks twice.)

❾ The *potters* . . . only threw *their* clay . . . (Breeding shows.)

❿ correct (So stuff it!)

BOTTOM LINE: "They/their" always applies to more than one:

a pinwheel	it/its
three cannons	they/their
Jerry	he/his
Mrs. Seinfeld	she/her
George and Elaine	they/their

If It

Was Me . . .

"If Old King Cole were to sing like Nat . . ."
"If Bela Lugosi were truly a bat . . ."
"But, *if it WAS ME . . .*" won't ever fly.
It's "*if it WERE I . . .*"—please remember that!

And when we muse about fanciful, hypothetical things, things that just don't exist, we have to use "were."

Examples

➤ If the farmer's wife were a compassionate woman, she wouldn't have mutilated those poor little mice last night.

➤ "If I were you," said one Watergate security guard to the other, "I'd go check some doors."

➤ If he were alone on a desert island, he'd feel a lot different about going steady.

You can also use "*as if*" and "*as though*" in the same way.

Examples

➤ Look at him strut. Prince Macaroni walks around *as if he were* king.

➤ As *if it were* any of her business in the first place, Darlene said Andre Agassi was too short for Brooke Shields.

➤ Marcel Marceau acts *as though* he were incapable of speaking his mind.

➤ Jody entered the room in that see-through negligee *as though* she were zipped up in a sleeping bag.

POINTED TIP: When "if" means "whether or not"—indicating the possibility of something existing—some people say use either "was" or "were." I side with those who say use "*was*."

Examples

"*If*" as in "*whether or not*":

➤ It didn't matter if (whether or not) Ada was able to sing "I Left My Heart in San Francisco"; they were casting *A Streetcar Named Desire*.

➤ Gutzon Borglum probably couldn't tell if (whether or not) he was carving Teddy Roosevelt's nose right until he stepped back from Mount Rushmore for a quick look.

➤ Ezio looked forward to walking a tightrope between the World Trade Center towers, which made one wonder if (whether or not) his brain was in the "on" position.

Quick Quiz

Circle the correct choice(s) in each of the following:

1. "I didn't know if I (was/were) coming or going in that thing," said H. G. Wells.
2. "After I told Romeo to go ahead with the wedding plans," said the oracle's priestess, "I wondered if he (was/were) going to tip me."
3. "If I (was/were) you, I'd put another couple of bricks on that side to keep it straight," said Tonio. But the mason of Pisa replied, "It's my tower. Butt out."
4. "Excuse me, sir, if I (was/were) to take a left here, would I find the Fountain of Youth?" asked Ponce de Leon.
5. "I'll say this for Lizzie Borden," said Mme de Farge while knitting a turtleneck sweater, "she didn't look as if she (was/were) the kind who'd hack up her folks and then sit down to a surf-and-turf special."
6. "I'd feel a lot better if Nathan (was/were) a little more experienced in this spying business," said Grandma Hale.
7. "If Al Pacino (was/were) willing to settle down here, we'd make a perfect couple," thought Renée as she slipped *Godfather II* into the VCR.
8. "I didn't know if Pembrooke (was/were) partial to gila monsters," said Halcyon, "so I kept Mr. Lizard in the bedroom until dessert."

Answers

❶ **was** (Wells was pointing to his time machine.)
❷ **was** (It turned out Romeo had very deep pockets, and very short arms.)
❸ **were** (The mason was cockeyed, so everything he built was slightly off.)
❹ **were** (The native said, "Yes," and then offered to sell Ponce the marsh we now call Disney World, but Ponce was too smart for him.)

❺ **were** (And Idi Amin had a nice smile.)
❻ **were** (They're *still* telling Nana Hale that Nathan's away at a "Final Words They'll Remember" seminar.)
❼ **were** (Sure.)
❽ **was** (Hey, Pembrooke, you forgot your hat!)

BOTTOM LINE: "If I *were* you," Old King Cole told Itzhak Perlman, "I'd start fiddling around." And Itzhak wondered *if* the king *was* going to bore him silly again with that story about the old fiddlers three, who suddenly joined Local 802 and refused to play for less than scale.

Location Is Everything

Picture a newsstand with magazines displayed according to subject: fitness and health, sports, current affairs, etc. Now, let's say a magazine called—no, wait. Make it a video store. Guy walks in and says to the clerk: "Where can I find 'The Art of Lovage'?"

"The art of loving?"

"No, lovage. L-o-v-a-g-e."

Clerk jerks his head. "Back there. Aisle D."

But Aisle D turns out to house videos of women in unusual positions with no clothes on. The guy wants a cassette about lovage, which is an herb . . . no, that doesn't work, either.

Look. *Where* words *are* in a sentence determines the meaning of the sentence.

Example

Take what I wrote above: "But Aisle D turns out to house videos of women in unusual positions with no clothes on." The *women* have no clothes on, not the *positions*. It's much better to say, "Aisle D turns out to house videos of women with no clothes on in unusual positions." And much better, in the end, to rent *Pocahontas*. (Must you always be titillated?)

More Examples

➤ As a child, my mom overindulged Dirk, who still won't lift a finger to rinse the sink after he shaves.

Think about it. "As a *child*, my *mom* . . ." That indicates that when *mom* was a *child*, she overindulged her son. Some trick.

Clear Intent: Since my mom overindulged Dirk as a child, *he* still won't lift . . .

➤ Cornelius said Juanita's accusations, flying to Chicago yesterday, were "sewer debris."

Who was flying to Chicago, Cornelius or Juanita's accusations?

Clear Intent: Flying to Chicago, *Cornelius* said . . .

➤ Emilio laughed uncontrollably at the rumor that he no longer loved Babette on TV.

Come on. The *rumor* was on TV, not Emilio and Babette in a clinch on top of the console.

Clear Intent: Emilio laughed uncontrollably at the rumor on TV that he no longer . . .

The tendency to put things in the wrong place is very understandable. It's what I think of as "the missing Jerome." In your mind, the words you're writing apply to "Jerome." You, of course, know that. *But if you don't stick those words near him, much less even mention him, how's a reader to know?* We're not mind readers, you know. From now on, take a few seconds to make sure you put "Jerome" where he belongs.

Quick Quiz

If there's a "Jerome" missing in any of the following sentences ("if"—ha! ha!), rewrite the sentence to put him in his place:

1. Once Mira got started, she let Clayton have it with everything she had that required a week at a health spa to recuperate.
2. After auditioning in full regalia as Lawrence of Arabia, the director decided to give Clayton a shot.
3. "As an idiot, I wonder what you think you're doing?" Ingrid remarked as Wilkins sprang out at her dressed like Howdy Doody.
4. "And here," said the curator gaily, "we have an example of art made by Pre-Columbian Indians in Gallery Four."
5. Driving over the bridge, Mathilda's carryall, kiln, and portable water bed fell off the luggage rack.
6. If convicted of bigamy, the jury will give Bluebeard what for.
7. At the reception, flushed and jubilant, the photographer snapped the bride.
8. Prone to spontaneous combustion, Dr. Lovejoy was astonished when Mrs. Gristede burst into flame.
9. For only $14.95, enjoy "Cafe Curtains: Problem Solvers or Strictly Window Dressing?" for a limited time only.
10. Sullenly, the tour guide led the group up to Grant's Tomb.

Answers

❶ Once Mira got started, she let Clayton have it with everything she had, and he required a week at a health spa to recuperate. (Everything *Mira had* didn't require a week to recuperate; Clayton did, and considering what he did, he's lucky she didn't try to lop off Mr. Dingle while she was at it.)

161

❷ After auditioning in full regalia as Lawrence of Arabia, Clayton won the part. (The director was not exactly averse to dolling up now and then, but *Clayton* was the one auditioning for the part of Lawrence of Arabia. . . . Clayton had nothing to lose: After his run-in with Mira, he was walking around in loose caftans, anyway.)

❸ "What kind of idiot are you, anyway?" remarked Ingrid as Wilkins sprang out dressed like Howdy Doody. (Surely, you can see that Wilkins was the idiot, not Ingrid.)

❹ "And here, in Gallery Four," said the curator gaily, "we have an example of Pre-Columbian Indian art." (If there were Indians who predated Columbus, making art in Gallery IV, the museum could charge some entrance fee.)

❺ While Mathilda was driving over the bridge, her carryall, kiln, and portable water bed fell off the luggage rack. (While her carryall, etc., were driving over the bridge, I suppose Mathilda was napping in the backseat, so I have no idea what fell off the luggage rack.)

❻ If convicted of bigamy, Bluebeard will have gotten it good from the jury. (*Bluebeard*, not the *jury*, is at risk of being convicted of bigamy. Actually, he was innocent. He didn't marry—or kill—more than one wife at a time. But, then, that's criminal justice for you. Slip up six, seven times and they figure you're guilty of everything.)

❼ At the reception, the photographer snapped the bride, who was flushed and jubilant. (The photographer did knock back a few when no one was looking, but in this instance, the *bride* was flushed and jubilant.)

❽ Prone to spontaneous combustion, Mrs. Gristede astonished Dr. Lovejoy when she burst into flames. (Honestly, do you think Dr. Lovejoy could have afforded his stable of stallions if he kept flaming up in front of patients? Mrs. Gristede was the "bright light.")

❾ Enjoy "Cafe Curtains: Problem Solvers or Strictly Window Dressing?" for only $14.95, for a limited time only. (The $14.95 is what's available for a limited time only, not your enjoyment of the brochure, although the narrative does wind down eventually.)

⑩ Actually, this one's okay. (How would you *have* the guide behave? It's a *tomb*, for cryin' out loud!)

POINTED TIP: *Where* one single word stands can also affect your meaning. For instance,

➤ Jock *often* said he would agree to dance the tarantella, if the New York Jets ever won.
➤ Jock said he would *often* agree to dance the tarantella, if the New York Jets ever won.

In sentence one, we have Jock often saying he'd make a fool of himself—*one time only*—given the (fat) chance. In sentence two, we have Jock saying he'd dance himself silly.

BOTTOM LINE: To make sure you're saying exactly what you mean, ask yourself, "Is it is or is it ain't where it belongs?" It's like giving directions. *Be precise*. There's no point telling Rheinhold to meet you at 46th Street and 7th Avenue, if you end up on 47th Street and 6th Avenue (unless you're trying to start an argument, so you can ditch him: "You never listen to me! I said 47th and Sixth!")

The Spy Who

Came in with

a Cold

"After you." The overseer held the door. Once inside, he removed Miles's handcuffs.

Soothing his wrists, Miles surveyed the room: minibar, sectional couch, home entertainment center. He cleared his throat, which felt raw.

Miles entered the kitchen. He glanced inside the refrigerator, then, lifting an eyebrow, faced the overseer. "I am the enemy. Have you forgotten?" He sneezed.

The overseer inclined his head. "Enjoy the evening, Mr. Rutherford," he said and left, locking the door behind him.

Miles was sitting down to a meal of baba ganoush and ouzo when he became aware of sibilance, as if a tape had been turned on. Raising his fork to his lips, he heard a strident female voice:

"... so then I said, look, ya *shoulda came* with us. ..."

Miles's hand froze in midair.

"... so he said, I *woulda went* with ya, but I had this appointment ..."

Miles's sinuses were pounding. He put down the fork and loosened his tie; the voice seemed to be coming from everywhere. He looked around but couldn't locate the speakers.

"... well, ya *shoulda saw* the look on his face when ..."

With trembling fingers, Miles unscrewed his nasal spray, but the suicide capsule was gone. Damn the overseer!

"... if he'd *a went* to my mom's, like I wanted ..."

Miles fell to the ground. He covered his ears, drew himself up into a ball, and began to scream, pausing only to cough. He was shivering.

In a room down the hall, where he was monitoring Miles's behavior on a screen, the overseer motioned to an aide. "Give Mr. Rutherford a moment of silence. Then pipe in the *Hee Haw* sound-tracks."

The overseer sat back and smiled. It wouldn't be long now!

What do you want? A trip to Branson, Missouri? It's yours, only puh-leez don't say:

came
went
saw

when what you want is

has/have/had come; should have/would have come
has/have/had gone; should have/would have gone
has/have/had seen; should have/would have seen

➤ You should have *seen* the look on Leona's face when they locked her in the slammer.
➤ You should have *seen* the look on King Minos' face when his wife gave birth to a son who was half boy, half bull (and not just in the symbolic sense).

➤ You should have *seen* Michael Jackson's faces.

➤ "Believe me, I would have *gone* another way," Hannibal said, "but over the Alps was the only route in those days."

➤ "I don't know if George M. Cohan has ever *gone* 'Over There,' " Mrs. Gershwin told George. "Don't talk while you're eating. You'll fill up on air."

➤ "I told him, '*Sherry's* husband would have *gone* to the Taj Mahal more than once if he'd had the chance.' But Joel just grunted and said, 'What do you want from me? I came. I saw the building. I'm going home.' "

➤ Owen has not really *come* to the lecture to learn about macramé. But then neither has Inez.

➤ "I would have *come* sooner," said Godot, "but I don't have to tell you what traffic is like on a Sunday."

➤ "We have *come* to bury Caesar. Get out of the way."

In your spare time, gaze at the following until it's plastered to the inside of your eyeballs:

I came. I have come. I had come. I would have come. I should have come. I shall have come.

We came. We have come. We had come. We would have come. We should have come. We shall have come.

You came. You have come. You had come. You would have come. You should have come. You will have come.

He/she came. He/she has come. He/she had come. He/she would have come. He/she should have come. He/she will have come.

They came. They have come. They had come. They would have come. They should have come. They will have come.

I saw. I have seen. I had seen. I would have seen. I should have seen. I shall have seen.

We saw. We have seen. We had seen. We would have seen. We should have seen. We shall have seen.

You saw. You have seen. You had seen. You would have seen. You should have seen. You will have seen.

He/she saw. He/she has seen. He/she had seen. He/she would have seen. He/she should have seen. He/she will have seen.

They saw. They have seen. They had seen. They would have seen. They should have seen. They will have seen.

I went. I have gone. I had gone. I would have gone. I should have gone. I shall have gone.

We went. We have gone. We had gone. We would have gone. We should have gone. We shall have gone.

You went. You have gone. You had gone. You would have gone. You should have gone. You will have gone.

He/she went. He/she has gone. He/she had gone. He/she would have gone. He/she should have gone. He/she will have gone.

They went. They have gone. They had gone. They would have gone. They should have gone. They will have gone.

Still with me?

Quick Quiz

Circle the correct choice(s) in each of the following:

1. "Drat. I should have (went/gone) for a haircut before I went riding," said Lady Godiva.
2. "When you've (saw/seen) one burning bush, you've (saw/seen) them all," Moses said casually.
3. "She should have (came/come) to the fair with us," said Anne Boleyn's mom. "Then maybe she wouldn't have lost her head over Henry the Eighth."
4. "I never would have (went/gone) out sailing on the *Pequod* in the first place, if I'd known how Ahab felt about whales," said Ishmael.
5. "Neil," said Mrs. Armstrong, "I wish you had (came/come) to the planetarium instead of playing with your model airplanes. Who knows if you'll ever see such good pictures of the moon again?"
6. "Mr. Hoffa told me he'd be right back. I don't know where he has (went/gone)."
7. Elvis never (saw/seen) a bangle he didn't like.

8. "Orville and Wilbur had work on their minds twenty-four hours a day," recalled Mrs. Wright fondly. "They never (came/come) to dinner on time."

9. After they had (saw/seen) *Cats* for the seventh time, Amy and Rob spit, uh, split up.

10. Just because no one ever (saw/seen) Dr. Jekyll and Mr. Hyde together doesn't necessarily mean they were one and the same. Kermit never (went/gone) to the studio without Jim Henson. Does that mean he couldn't breathe without him?

11. "What do you mean, 'I should have (saw/seen) it coming'!" cried Noah as the water rose above his shoulders.

12. "We should have (went/gone) bowling with the pigs," Hansel told Gretel as he brushed off the crumbs.

Answers

❶ **gone** (Actually, a few bobby pins would have done the job just as well.)

❷ **seen, seen** (Oh, sure. And rivers split down the middle every day of the week.)

❸ **come** (Henry VIII loved to see tongues wag and heads roll.)

❹ **gone** (It always pays to ask questions up front.)

❺ **come** (I guess Neil showed her!)

❻ **gone** (When he said that, the guy had a strange, faraway look in his eye, you know?)

❼ **saw** (Or a car, a sandwich, a pill . . .)

❽ **came** (I heard Mrs. Wright complained plenty about their behavior before they got off the ground.)

❾ **seen** (I'm a dog person, myself.)

❿ **saw, went** (What kind of fool do you take me for, anyway?)

⓫ **seen** (There were actually two Noahs. This was the first.)

⓬ **gone** ("Should have," "would have"—what's done is done. Take a hike!)

BOTTOM LINE: Even if they threaten you with 112 episodes of *Married . . . with Children* back to back, don't ever say, "I have came," "you should have went," or "he would have saw." It's "*I have come. You should have gone. He would have seen.*"

THE GRAMMATICALLY CORRECT HANDBOOK
THE GRAMMATICALLY CORRECT HANDBOOK
THE GRAMMATICALLY CORRECT HANDBOOK
THE GRAMMATICALLY CORRECT HANDBOOK
THE GRAMMATICALLY CORRECT HANDBOOK
THE GRAMMATICALLY CORRECT HANDBOOK
THE GRAMMATICALLY CORRECT HANDBOOK
THE GRAMMATICALLY CORRECT HANDBOOK

3

Miscellaneous

Misunderstandings

(Hmm...)

Feel Bad/ Feel Badly

There were three blind men, and one day they ended up in a room they'd never been in before. Pretty soon, they became aware they weren't alone. There was a creature of some sort in there with them. It was an elephant, but since the men were blind, they didn't know that.

The first man put out his hand and touched the elephant's trunk. "Hey, fellas, I think what we've got here is a snake."

"Don't be ridiculous," said the second man, who had the elephant by the leg. "It's a rhino."

"You guys are both nuts," said the third man, who was holding the elephant's ear. "This is a sea mammal of some sort, probably a manatee."

Just then, the door opened and the trainer walked in. "All right, break it up," he said, leading the elephant out. "We've got a show to put on."

When the three blind men found out it was an elephant after all, they all felt bad. Eventually, though, they all insisted they had not *felt* badly at all, considering that each of them had only felt a part of the whole thing.

Moral: To "feel bad" means any or all of the following:

➤ You realize too late that you *should* have chosen number four on that multiple choice question about amino acids;

➤ You're sorry you only sprang for a Mother's Day card, since your brother-the-toad also sent chocolates;

➤ You were unhappy when Mrs. Quayle's husband lost his job (what's he doing, by the way?).

To "feel badly" means

➤ either your emotional mechanism is fouled up (and Debra Winger's deathbed farewell to her sons in *Terms of Endearment* has you convulsed with laughter),

➤ or your sense of touch needs adjusting (you can't distinguish a honeydew from a bowling ball).

Quick Quiz

Circle the correct choice(s) in each of the following:

1. In *La Boheme,* Rodolpho felt (bad/badly) when Mimi began to cough.
2. John Hancock didn't feel (bad/badly) when the other delegates to the Continental Congress hollered at him for taking up half the page with his signature.
3. The great Yogi Guppy had spectacular success on the lecture circuit because he could teach people how not to feel (bad/badly). However, he couldn't model clay for spit, because he always felt (bad/badly).

4. Nobody felt (bad/badly) for the hunchback of Notre Dame except Esmeralda.

5. Travis was a failure at finger puppets because he felt (bad/badly).

Answers

❶ **bad** (Mimi never covered her mouth when she hacked.)

❷ **bad** (Once he was out of there, John Hancock didn't plan on seeing any of those guys again anyway.)

❸ **bad, badly** (People are so judgmental.)

❹ **bad** (Nice girl, but no saint. Did you ever see her sharing a mutton leg with him after church? I rest my case.)

❺ **badly** (Travis did fine with Mr. Pinky, but he never got the hang of Rosie Ring Finger.)

BOTTOM LINE: Barbra Streisand will *feel bad* if you rain on her parade; if Greek worry beads don't cure Old Mother Hubbard's anxiety about her dog, it's because she *feels badly*.

Hopefully

I wish I may, I wish I might
straighten this out, once and for all.

Hopefully, Theron guided Constanza toward the bedroom.

The marquis hopefully watched the roulette wheel spin, since he owned the casino.

B. Knighted hopefully submitted his name to the Smart Persons Society.

Translated

With great hope in his heart, Theron guided Constanza toward the bedroom.

The marquis watched the roulette wheel optimistically . . .

B. Knighted was full of hope when he submitted his name to the Smart Persons Society, but it turned out those dummies aren't as smart as they'd like us to think they are!

HOPEFULLY is a veritable bouquet of hope!

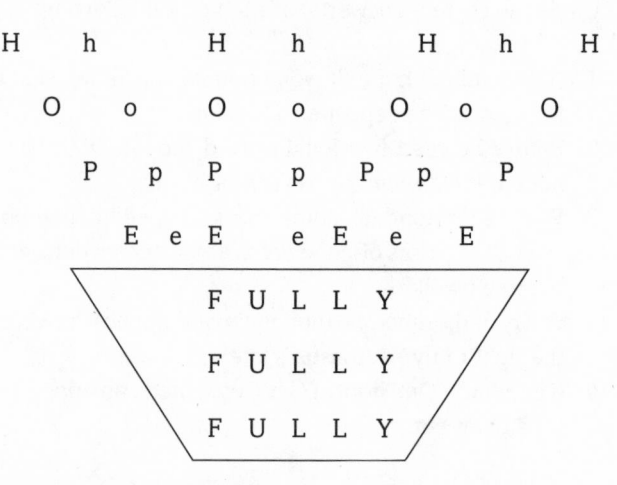

However, when you say,

➤ Hopefully, I'll be rid of my eczema by next month;
➤ Hopefully, the tape won't break when Forest Hills records his blackmailer;
➤ Hopefully, Portia will live to complain another day,

there is a smidgen of doubt in that "hopefully," an iota of concern and anxiety.

In these instances, what you're really trying to say is

➤ *I hope* I'll be rid of my eczema by next month.
➤ *It is to be hoped* that the tape won't break when Forest Hills records his blackmailer.
➤ *One hopes* that Portia will live to complain another day.

In other words, do not confuse "hopefully" with "I hope, you hope, we all hope, one hopes, it is to be hoped," and "Please, dear God, give me this one, and I'll find a way to make it up to you."

Quick Quiz

Circle the correct answer(s) in each of the following:

1. "(Hopefully/I hope) it won't bounce this time," said Mrs. Morgan as she deposited J.P.'s check.
2. Before he read it, Mocking Bird (hopefully/it is to be hoped) kissed *Variety*'s review of his act.
3. When Ada Rondack comes back, (hopefully/one hopes) she will have lots of good yarns about her adventures with the tree dwellers.
4. Purity and Brimstone (hopefully/it is hoped) drew lots for the right to fly Al Abaster's kite.
5. (Hopefully/One hopes) Gar Goyle made an appointment for a blunt cut.

Answers

❶ **I hope** (Not all Morgans named J.P. are rolling in it.)
❷ **hopefully** (*Variety* said, "No Big 'Trill.'")
❸ **one hopes** (Ada yaks you to death even when her stories stink.)
❹ **hopefully** (I don't have a clue. Draw your own conclusions.)
❺ **hopefully** (No amount of talking could convince Gar that, given the shape of his face, layering was best.)

BOTTOM LINE: "Hopefully, Pelham and Parkway exchanged vows of togetherness. Interstate 95 hopes things work out for them."

Loan/ Lend

"**I** don't know how I done it," Lila said excitedly. "First, Fred calls to say he wants to come over and talk, and I yawn and say, 'Yeah.' "

"Did he, like, apologize?" asked Allegra, twining her hair around her finger.

"Hold on, would ya?" Lila retorted. "So he comes over and I'm like real laid-back and he says, 'Since it looks like we're broke up, I wanna return the twenty dollars you lent me for brunch that Sunday—' "

"Whadya say?"

"So I says, 'Forget it. I'll give you back the American Gladiators sweatshirt you loaned me last year, and we'll, like, call it quits and—"

"So did ya?"

Lila slapped the table. "You gonna let me tell this or what?" She took a long pause. Then, "So Fred says, 'Hey, keep it. It looks good on ya,' and then he touches me on the cheek, real tenda like and—"

Yatata, yatata, yatata. Lila and Fred are getting married next year. Neither of them used "loan" and "lend" with precision, but what the hell? As long as they're happy. . . .

If you're a stickler, there's only one real difference between "loan" and "lend." Money. For instance, not only would Ogden *loan* Wilt a twenty every week, he would also *lend* him his microwave and his street map of Luxembourg.

"Loan" usually only goes with money (along with grief); "lend" can go with money, plus everything else.

So Fred should have said, "I wanna return the twenty dollars you *loaned* me . . ." And Lila should have said, "I'll give you back the American Gladiators sweatshirt you *lent* me . . ." And Allegra should have kept her mouth shut altogether.

BOTTOM LINE: If you want to split hairs, "lend" Bianca your original recording of "Penny Lane," but don't "loan" her a cent.

F A R

FARTHER

Even Farther

From "far" comes "farther." Both are concerned with miles, feet, yards, inches, kilometers, and anything else that denotes "distance."

"Further" means "more," "extra," in the sense that there's more involved.

"Furthermore" means "in addition to," "plus which," "besides," "what's more," and like that there.

Examples

➤ Istanbul is just as far from Tanzania now as it was when it was called Constantinople.

➤ "How much farther is it to Grandma's house?" asked Little Red Riding Hood. The wolf shrugged. "Half a mile or so. Here, honey, let me carry that for you."

➤ "I'm looking forward to further exploration of the sun," Mr. Icarus told Channel 2 from his bed in the intensive care unit.

➤ "Any further fooling around and you're off the ark," Mrs. Noah warned the hyenas.

➤ Furthermore, you get unlimited trips to the salad bar, but you've got to make a deposit on the time share right now.

➤ "I pledge, furthermore, not to take any money from special interests that don't contribute to me!"

POINTED TIP: You *can* say, "Derek will go far in psycholinguistic training," meaning that he'll be successful and make a lot of money from people who think he knows what he's talking about. We say, "She or he will go far" in this way because that's what we do.

Quick Quiz

Circle the correct choice(s) in each of the following:

1. "Until (farther/further) notice, these premises are off-limits," St. Peter said, and slammed the Pearly Gates on Mr. Murdoch.

2. "Look, lady, I got nothin' to do with how the meter works," said the cabbie. "It ain't just the (further/farther) you go, the more you pay. It also costs for sittin' at lights, makin' turns, and goin' around Columbus Circle four, five times."

3. (Further/farther) evidence linking Henry David Thoreau to water pollution arose tonight, when graduate students excavating Walden Pond brought up a cache of candles burned at both ends. They bore the message, "To Hank: Thanks for the memories. Emily Dickinson."

4. "I won't fly any (further/farther) without lunch!" hollered Ensign Benson, and he brought the spaceship to a halt outside the 7-Eleven on Alpha Newt.

5. All (further/farther) inquiries regarding refunds should be addressed to Make $100,000 in Your Spare Time Writing Jingles!, c/o ConArts, Inc., Tierra del Fuego.

6. (Furthermore/In addition), white patent leather perfectly accessorizes this year's abundance of pastels.

Answers

❶ **further** (Murdoch's case was referred to the Arbitrating Angels Commission, in which he holds a 52 percent interest.)

❷ **farther** (I think they call this type of personality "colorful." It's just about extinct.)

❸ **further** (Hey! They were human! They had needs!)

❹ **farther** (Ensign Benson will not "go far" in space.)

❺ **further** (You can do way better addressing envelopes.)

❻ **furthermore** or **in addition** (Don't *ever* use "accessorize," though, unless *Vogue* is paying you to.)

BOTTOM LINE: You can't go *farther* than California without hitting water. *Furthermore*, the farther west you go, the *further* your chances of ending up back where you started.

On Good

Speaking

Terms

The sun was just rising as Sable pulled onto the expressway. She slipped the cassette into the tape deck and pressed "play":

"Greetings. This is lesson one. We'll be reviewing commonly mispronounced words and learning how to say them correctly. Take a deep breath."

Sable inhaled.

"Now, repeat after me: I *oft*en skip meals. *Off*-en. Silent t."

"I should *oft*en skip meals," said Sable.

"Nothing is *com*parable to an iced tea on a hot day."

"Nothing is *com*parable to a quart of ice cream on a hot day." Sable was driving in the middle lane at a moderate speed, when she became aware that an eighteen-wheeler was gaining on her. Within seconds, he was inches from her bumper.

"*Ex*pletive deleted was a common phrase in the seventies."

"*Ex*pletive deleted stands for @#!% ^*!" Sable glared at the truck in her rearview mirror and held her speed.

"Compromise is *pre*ferable to combat."

The truck driver blasted his horn, but Sable held fast. "Combat is *pre*ferable to compromise," she said, "and you've got two free lanes to pass me in, buster. Use one!"

"People frequently behave inex*plic*ably."

The truck driver glued his hand to his horn.

"Neanderthal men often behave inex*plic*ably!" hollered Sable. The horn was deafening, and she increased the volume of the cassette player.

"What's *ap*plicable in one situation may not be in another."

Sable took a moment. "I do believe this is *ap*plicable." All at once, she hit her brakes.

Caught off guard, the trucker stomped on his brakes and veered into the right lane, cutting off a speeding Porsche, whose owner swerved the wheel, and stopped short on the shoulder of the road.

Eyeing them in her rearview mirror—they were irate but unhurt—Sable whooped and pumped her fist. She accelerated and took the next exit off the expressway.

"Many people aspire to be *af*fluent," said the tape.

"Mess with me and you'd better be *af*fluent and highly insured," Sable muttered.

"Mr. Smith appreciated the *min*uscule things in life."

Sable slowed for a stoplight and rolled her shoulders, easing the tension in her back. "The *min*uscule gives me satisfaction, too."

She made a turn and pulled into one of the reserved parking spaces in front of the municipal building.

"Mr. Smith did not have a *do*ur disposition. That's *do*-er, not *dow*-er."

"*Do*-er, *do*-er." Sable shifted into park and checked her watch. The tape played on.

"Column A and column B are *dis*parate—*dis*parate, not dis*par*ate."

"And column C is the most *dis*parate of all," said Sable.

"Mr. Smith was a connoisseur of diamonds—con-no-*sir*, '*sir*' as in 'were,' not con-no-*sewer*."

"As a con-no-*sir* of diamonds, Mr. Smith knew hot rocks when he saw them," Sable said.

"Mrs. Smith wanted to vacation at the Fontaine*bleau*—the phone-ten-*blow*, not fahn-ten-*blew*."

"If Mr. Smith takes his wife to the Phone-ten-*blow*," Sable said, "he'd better do it with clean money."

"Mr. Smith is not a saboteur—sa-bo-*tir*, '*tir*' as in '*her*.' He is an entrepreneur—ahn-tre-pre-*nir*, '*nir*,' also as in '*her*.' "

"Good for Mr. Smith." Sable turned off the ignition, switched the cassette to her portable player, put on the headphones, and left the car. She hurried toward the municipal building.

"Nothing is ir*rev*ocable."

"Just about everything is ir*rev*ocable," sputtered Sable as she tackled the first of three flights of stairs that rose to the majestic entrance of the building.

"Juanita had a *burge*oning career; bur-jon-ing, soft 'g' sound, as in *Gibraltar*, not 'burgening,' as in 'hamburger.' "

"Jua . . . Jua . . ." Sable gasped. She hadn't been to the health club in weeks.

Finally, she was outside the huge, ornate entrance. Collecting herself, she went in.

"Morning, Jock." She greeted the guard just inside.

"Morning, Judge," he responded, and touched the brim of his cap.

BOTTOM LINE: Inhale. Now:

often	*off*-en
comparable	*com*-parable
expletive	*ex*-pletive
preferable	*pref*-erable
inexplicably	inex-*pli*-cably
applicable	*ap*-plicable
affluent	*af*-fluent
minuscule	*min*-uscule
dour	*do*-ur
disparate	*dis*-parate
connoisseur	con-no-*sir*
Fontainbleau	*phone*-ten-*blow*
entrepreneur	ahn-tre-pre-*nir*
saboteur	sa-bo-*tir*
irrevocable	ir-*rev*-ocable
burgeoning	*burge*-oning (soft "g")

Sable was a *for*-midable (not for-*mid*-able) magistrate.

Penultimate

There once was a runner so fit,
During practice, he merely would sit.
So the day of the race,
He retired in disgrace,
After finishing penultimate.

Surprise! "Penultimate" means "next to last," not "better than best." Therefore, "That fettuccine was the penultimate!" *doesn't* mean it was the tastiest, most scrumptious pile of pasta you ever ate. It was the "next to last" thing you ate—right after the calamari and before the spumoni.

Here are a couple of ways to wash away the "super" image of penultimate from your brain:

➤ "Florence's cousin Alvin was the penultimate in looks" can be read as "Alvin had *such* a nice personality!"

➤ "Winston's collection of abstract masterpieces was the penultimate in taste" can be translated "Get a load of the garbage on *this* guy's walls. Only your brother-in-law's is crappier."

Quick Quiz

Choose the penultimate item in the following:

Monday

Tuesday

Wednesday

Thursday

Friday

Sunday

Saturday

Answer

Sunday

Don't blame me if you stopped reading after "Wednesday" and made assumptions. In *this* list, Sunday is next to last.

BOTTOM LINE: The penultimate straw comes next to last, right before the camel's back gives way.

Emerged:

How?

Choose the phrase or word that correctly finishes the thought, "Marcel emerged . . ."

Your choices are

1. victorious
2. on the scene
3. from the Hudson

Those of you who chose (1) or (2), take two steps back. Those of you who chose (1), (2), and (3), take three steps back. Those of you who chose (3), stay where you are.

Get a load of this: (3) is the only correct choice.

Now, those of you in the back, put your hands together and give Broderick, all alone up here, a great, big hand for getting it right.

"Emerge" means to come into view from someplace that *hid* you from view. I know that's the last meaning in the world the word has come to mean. And if you still want to say, "Avery *emerged*** quite snotty after winning at skee-ball," or, "Lester *emerged* as a fresh voice at this year's hog-calling competition," be my guest.

If, however, you want to hold your head high and be able to look yourself in the eye, use "emerge" in its unperverted sense, as in

➤ On Groundhog Day, the groundhog *emerged* bleary-eyed and twenty pounds overweight.

➤ The minute the sword Excalibur *emerged* from the lake in which it had been submerged, King Arthur grabbed it.

➤ When Gertrude *emerged* from her cave, she was covered with stalagmites (or possibly stalactites).

*emerged, as in "became"

BOTTOM LINE: When you "emerge," you come out, come out, from wherever you are!

How Can
You Say
That?

The Morning Dispatch

Town Notes and Quotes
by Gwynneth String

Believe it or not, today is Lamar Genzel's 104th birthday! I know we all wish him the happiest of birthdays yet. We're so proud of him.

I bumped into his daughter, Ina, yesterday, and she said, "Silverware would not be where it is today without Papa. He was a pioneer. Thanks to him, there are left-handed forks. That little invention really *impacted* our whole way of life. We had money falling out of our ears. Papa *input* all his energies into making eating easier for the digitally challenged. And he *accessed* some of the best-known left-handers in the country for endorsements."

As you know, there's going to be a big celebration tonight for Lamar at the Left-Handed Compliments Center. If you haven't gotten your ticket yet, Ina tells me some are still available. Remember, it's for a good cause. We're *looking* to use the proceeds to lobby for left-handed stamps.

The English language is always changing. What was unacceptable during the Stone Age has become perfectly routine.

I know, I know.

But what, I ask, is so terrible about a little continuity?

And don't hand me the argument that I myself have broken, and continue to break, "the rules" by writing incomplete sentences and starting some of them with "and," "which," and "but," which used to be a no-no. I have Achilles tendons just like you. "But" (ha! ha!) if I live to be as old as Lamar, I won't be able to hear someone say, "Can you *access* the witchit?" without experiencing an impulse to rip the speaker's throat out.

"Access" and the other words highlighted in Gwynneth's column are jargon.

- ➤ access, impact, input: computer speak
- ➤ look to (like "coming off of"): sports speak

These words and phrases have been corrupted, defaced, bent and broken, distorted, and yes, led astray from their original intents.

They have been defiled!

So? So, this: You can say "access witchits" as much as you want. But how about *also* using "access," "impact," "input," etc., as they were groomed to be used when they were young and pure?

For example,

- ➤ Zoltan longed for access to Jasmine's closet.
- ➤ "But how will we gain access to Professor Vidablue's truffles?" queried Merlynne.
- ➤ Punkin's gift for sweet talk had a phenomenal impact on her career at Consolidated Condiments.

➤ When the community got wind of Haskell's hostility toward herring, the impact on his social standing was astonishing.

➤ "Since you contributed no input during the open-mike session, we do not want to hear your views on Day-Glo as a mood enhancer now!" cried Parker.

➤ Rory's creative input during the rehearsal of "Knots, Nots, and Noes: A Philosophical Fugue" consisted of "Do that part again."

"Look/looking to" is an inane, exasperating way of saying, among others:

➤ I'm *striving to* see this expression carried out on its back, with its feet in the air.

➤ I *want to* drop a two-ton lid on this expression.

➤ I'm *desirous of* running a stake through the heart of this expression.

➤ I'm *eager to* shred this expression into landfill.

➤ I *hope to* knock the daylights out of this expression.

BOTTOM LINE: "Access," "impact," and "input" are not just single-minded soloists. They often appreciate accompanying words:

gain access to

have access to, etc.

the impact of something or other

had an impact on or upon, etc.

my input

your input

every annoying Jack and Jill's input

In your spare time, please give the cold shoulder to "look/looking to" and embrace "want to," "hope to," "plan to," "seek to," etc.

More (or Most) Important/More Importantly

The color of its feet enables observers to distinguish a red-footed from a blue-footed booby. Sinclair, however, felt it was *more important* to get out of the boobys' way when they were landing than to pay attention to which type was tumbling into him. *Most important,* Sinclair was eager to ditch the whole population survey and get back to Mayberry.

There. You use "more important" to show that something or someone is of more value than something or someone else. And you also use "more important" (not "more important*ly*") to indicate you're on the verge of pointing that out.

Examples

➤ Florenz felt it was more important for the critics to say good things about his "Follies" than to spell his name right. (Once and for all, it's Ziegfeld, not Ziegfield.)

➤ "Forget about how you spell 'Mpingo,'" said Perkins. "More important, the tree is becoming extinct. Once it is, what'll we use for clarinets?"

BOTTOM LINE: The residents of Hamelin felt it was important to get rid of the rats. *More important,* they hated to pay the Pied Piper what they owed him once he'd cleaned out the vermin. *Most important,* in the end, though, they had underestimated the piper's capacity for revenge when rubes like them stiffed him.

Former/
Latter/
Later

Y ou need two things, or people, in order to use "former" and "latter." "Former" refers to the first one, the one that comes before the other. "Latter" refers to the one that comes *after* the one that comes before.

"Later," with one "t," means, "Not now! I'm watching *E.R.*"

For instance, Catherine the Great (former) was not Catherine I (latter). The *former* ran Russia from 1762 until 1796, which may be why she was considered great. The *latter* had a much shorter run, from 1725 until 1727. In the end, Catherine the Great was actually Catherine II, and she came *later* than Catherine I.

Quick Quiz

Fill in former and latter in each of the following:

1. Ethelbad was the son of Ethelwulf. They both ruled England during the ninth century.

former _____
latter _____

2. Basically, you've got two kinds of trees: deciduous and evergreen.

former _____
latter _____

3. No doubt, the two most famous Heidis are Heidi of the Alps and Heidi Fleiss of Hollywood.

former _____
latter _____

4. Ethan Allen had a brother named Ira.

former _____
latter _____

Answers

❶ **Ethelbad (former), Ethelwulf (latter)** (Ethelbad had two brothers, Ethelbert and Ethelred. I like to think there was an Ethelmertz somewhere in the family, too.)

❷ **deciduous (former), evergreen (latter)** (Trees in the former group lose their leaves each year; those in the latter are emotionally needier and hang on to theirs.)

❸ Heidi of the Alps (former), Heidi Fleiss of Hollywood (latter) (The former was a little orphan, sent to live with her grandfather; the latter, well, let's just say she had lots of "uncles.")

❹ Ethan Allen (former), Ira Allen (latter) (Ethan was in charge of the Green Mountain Boys in 1775. His brother Ira, a Green Mountain Boy, too, was later involved in politics. The former got caught by the British at one point, yet we still remember him more than the latter. Go figure.)

BOTTOM LINE: The "former" comes first; the "latter" comes "later."

Different From/
Different Than

I n a distant part of the temple . . .

goooooooooooooooooooooooooooooo

a gong sounded, its vibrations penetrating . . .

oooooooonnnnnnnnnnnnnnngggggggg

Dabney's very soul. He knocked his elbows together in the ritual greeting and murmured, "Mahamaven."

"You have come a long way, my son," the mahamaven said, adjusting his robe.

"From Palm Springs."

The mahamaven smiled broadly. "You don't happen to know Sonny Bono, do you? Or Meg and Emmett Schiff?"

Dabney shook his head.

The mahamaven recrossed his legs (it was murder on the joints, sitting like that). "You have braved many dangers to seek my counsel, my boy. What is it you wish to know?"

Dabney inched closer and recrossed *his* legs. "Why is one man's soul so *different from* another's?"

The mahamaven nodded. "What else do you wish to know?"

"How come when you remove shrink-wrap, nine times out of ten one little piece keeps sticking to your fingers? And, finally," Dabney said, his words coming quickly in his excitement, "what makes Ralph Polo's T-shirts any *different from* the three-for-ten-dollar variety they sell at flea markets?"

The mahamaven deliberated. Then he peered into Dabney's face with that riveting gaze of his. "Where are you staying? I'll get back to you."

The correct term is "different from," not "different than," no matter what.

> ➤ "If you can conceive it, you can do it" is quite *different from* "If you can conceive it, it must be cocky-poo."
> ➤ *The Side Street Most Taken* had a *different* sales record *from* that other book's.

BOTTOM LINE: No matter what you're comparing, nothing is *different than* anything else; everything, however, is *different from* everything else.

(N)**Ei**th**er**/

(N)**O**r

Parallel lines:

— —
— —

/ /

| |

\ \

Neither _____ nor
Either _____ or

DON'T CROSS THESE LINES!

If you start out with "neither," follow up with "nor." If you begin with "either," sign off with "or."

> *Neither* Hallie *nor* Harmony knew how to run interference.
> "He was *either* in it up to his neck *or* in Omaha as he claims," the sergeant declared.

You cannot say "neither _____ or"!

POINTED TIP: Feel free to use "neither," "either," "or," and "nor" on their own:

> **Neither** **was a baritone, so Punch and Judy took up the saxophone.**
> **"Leo, are you going to return these tapes, or are you going to sit there writing about war and peace forever?" asked Grandpa Tolstoy.**
> **Magna wasn't eager to hike, nor was she hot to trot.**
> **"I take honey or sugar with my gin," said Parnell. "Either will do."**

As far as Punch and Judy up above, you say, "Neither . . . *was*," not "neither . . . *were*," because what you mean is "neither *one* of them sang like Gordon MacRae. . . ."

Now—here we go again—to make sure things "agree" (see Let's Agree, Shall We?), you've got to balance the scales correctly. It all depends on what comes after "nor" and how many of them there are. For instance, if one lummox follows "nor," the drill is "nor . . . is/was/etc."

> *Neither* Hornsby *nor Duffy* (one) *was* willing to take part in the tutu extravaganza.

If several lummoxes come after "nor," it's "neither . . . nor . . . are/were/etc."

➤ *Neither* Butch Cassidy *nor* the other *delinquents* (several) *were* elegant models on the runway."

Quick Quiz

Circle the correct choice(s) in each of the following:

1. "Listen to me once and for all," Mother Wolf told her eldest cub. "Neither you (nor/or) your sister (is/are) ready to howl alone."
2. "Either you guys come out, (nor/or) I'm coming in after you," warned the anteater.
3. "I'm certain," said Luna. "The duchess (either/neither) wears flannel (nor/or) hats after July Fourth."
4. Neither the cotton swabs (or/nor) the pincushions (was/were) on Sebastian's "best-gift" list.

Answers

❶ **nor, is** (The cubs were eighteen and sixteen, respectively, from which we can infer that Mother Wolf was doing one hell of a job preparing them for "shrinkage" at a later date.)

❷ **or** (The anteater was always sticking his nose where it wasn't wanted.)

❸ **either/or, neither/nor** (Either way, the duchess has some dress code.)

❹ **nor, were** (Fine! Let him buy his own damn gifts!)

BOTTOM LINE: It's "neither _____ nor" and "either _____ or." And any of them on their own, as in: Cotton Mather looked out at his Puritan congregation. It was hot, and many of them had their sleeves rolled up. Cotton shot his cuffs, brought his arms out to his sides, and declared, "If I don't have the right to bare arms, *neither* do you!"

Words That

Aren't

"**G**randpa, tell me the story about the penguin."
Scottie climbed up on the old man's knee
and rested his head against his chest.

"Okay," Grandpa said and put down his pipe. "Once upon a time, there was a penguin named Floyd. He lived near the *Arctic* (1) with his best friend, a moose named Minna. All year long, they played together.

"First, though, Floyd and Minna would go foraging for food. *Regardless* (2) of the weather, Floyd always looked for fish in the sea, and Minna looked through the *foliage* (3) for things moose eat. And—"

"Get to the good part, Grandpa."

"Okay. Just then, the ogre tripped on a glacier and pulled a hamstring. He sat down, cursing. 'What have you got to say for yourself now?" cried Floyd. 'Don't tell me you're at a loss for words—you, who are known far and wide for your *verbiage* (4).'

" 'Can it!' hollered the ogre. 'Making fun of me in this situation is simply *indefensible* (5)!'

" 'Aw, give it a rest!' yelled Floyd. 'Ever since Minna accidentally let you out of that Express Mail package she found in the shrubs, you've been giving me nothing but bad dreams. Night after night, they *recur* (6). Now, maybe I'll get some rest!'

"The ogre, who had grown to a *height* (7) of twenty-seven feet just in the time he sat there rubbing his knee, let out a roar. 'Your attitude is absolutely *inexplicable* (8), and your *judgment* (9) warped. Am I not an ogre? Is not my hostility an *integral* (10) part of my nature?'

"He was about to go into his unhappy childhood when Minna popped up. 'Say, Floyd—the berries are ripe! You grab some shrimp and we'll have ourselves one sweet meal!' And off they ran, *dissociating* (11) themselves entirely from the ogre, who sat there, gnashing his tooth. Everybody, except him, lived happily ever after." Any other ending would have been *anticlimactic* (12).

The numbered words are correct. You can put that in the bank:

1. **Arctic** has a "c" before the "t" (the same is true for Antarctic); "Artic" is wrong.
2. **Regardless** doesn't come with an "ir" up front because you don't need it: "regardless" means without regard; "irregardless" would mean without-without regard; in other words, *with* regard.
3. **Foliage** For some reason, many horticulturists and gardeners leave out the "i" and go around saying, "folage." They're probably in a hurry to sow something. In any case, "foliage" is *spelled* as if it had three syllables, even if you slur the "i" when you say it: "fo-li-age."
4. **Verbiage** Ditto, regarding the "i." "Verbiage" is spelled as if it had three syllables, which it has: "verb-i-age."
5. **Indefensible** The prefix "un" is often used, but not in

front of "defensible": "*in*defensible" not "undefensible." (Same goes for "opportune": "inopportune" not "unopportune.")

6. **Recur** When they were writing the rules, they decided it was better to say "re-cur" than "reoccur." That rule still stands, and anyone who says otherwise can step outside with me and my friend Bull here.

7. **Height** ("hite") ends with a "t," not another "h." "Width" has the "h" at the end and the "thuh" sound. "Height" has a "t." "Heighth" doesn't exist.

8. **Inexplicable** You don't want "unexplainable." Believe me.

9. **Judgment** No "e" after the "g." No "e" after the "g." No "e" after the "g," damn it! (Except in Great Britain. . . .)

10. **Integral,** which means "essential," takes an "r" after the "g," not after the "t." "Intregal" means nothing whatsoever; "integral" means a lot.

11. **Dissociate,** not "disassociate." You "associate" yourself with whale watchers and chocoholics. You "dissociate" yourself from Hetty, who has developed an unhealthy interest in the polka.

12. **Anticlimactic:** This word comes from the word "climax," which refers to the aha! moment, the payoff, the culmination. If you leave out the second "c," you end up with "anticlimatic," which indicates negative feelings toward the weather.

POINTED TIP: This * is an "aster*isk*," not an "asterik." Think of "flask," instead of "flick," if that helps. If it doesn't, forget it.

BOTTOM LINE: These are the correct words:

1. "Arctic," not Artic
2. "regardless," not irregardless
3. "foliage," not folage
4. "verbiage," not verbage
5. "indefensible," not undefensible ("inopportune," not "unopportune")
6. "recur," not reoccur
7. "height," not heighth
8. "inexplicable," not unexplainable
9. "judgment," not judgement (Except in the United Kingdom, I said!)
10. "integral," not intregal
11. "dissociate," not disassociate
12. "anticlimactic," not anticlimatic

I've Heard That Song Before

S ome things get even better when they're repeated:

"Hi! Here's your check from Publishers Clearinghouse."
"Eunice, John Travolta is on the phone for you."
"The Nobel Committee wants to know when you can pick up
your prize."

Some words, though, only need to be said once:

➤ Don't say "*new* innovation." An *innovation*, in and of itself, is brand-new.

Example: The boys Romulus and Remus were brought up by a wolf, which was an *innovation* in parenting.

➤ Don't say "refer *back*" to. *Refer* just needs a "to."

Example: "Your Honor, I *refer* counsel to the previous testimony of his slimy client."

➤ Don't say "revert *back*," either. *Revert* actually means "go back," so just add a "to."

Example: The rights to Blake's collection of Doris Day CDs *revert* to Blake, if he outlives his frisky young wife Jezebel.

➤ Don't say "proceed *on*." *Proceed* only goes one way: forward, ahead, onward (like "continue").

Example: "Let's *proceed* to item seven. Belinda, how many enthusiasts have you signed up for the naked Ping-Pong tournament?"

➤ Don't say "reason *why*," or "reason . . . *because*." *Reason*, by itself, means "explanation."

Examples:

➤ The *reason* he put on his galoshes was unclear, since the sun was out.

➤ The *reason* Myrna dumped Darryl was his preoccupation with rubber bands.

➤ Don't say "fall off of." *Fall off*, as in topple over, needs no assistance.

Example: "When Tonto *fell off* Scout, he said something I can't repeat."

In fact, don't say "of" after "off" at all:

➤ Desiree couldn't keep her *eyes off* Wade's money market fund.

➤ Nolan liked to *surf off* Adelaide, until she made him get a board.

➤ As soon as Damon *came off* the disabled list, he got called for jury duty.

➤ Annie Oakley never *took her eye off* the target, even when Buffalo Bill was creeping up on her with that nasty grin on his face.

➤ Don't say "more unique." *Unique* means one of a kind. Period.

Example: Bella had a *unique* ability to detect unmarried men on the bus.

➤ Don't say, "The preacher was a hairy *one*," or "Ms. Poppins's history of unmade beds was a long and bothersome *one*." Do say, "The preacher was hairy," or "Ms. Poppins's history of unmade beds was long and bothersome."

One is best used when

➤ counting harpsichords (one, two, three)
➤ pointing out, "One of us is not from Kansas," or "The one who collects the most crickets cannot stay here tonight."
➤ using it elegantly, as the British do: "One doesn't want to infuriate oneself, does one?"

➤ Don't say "emotional anguish." *Anguish* can only be emotional.

Example: Grover's anguish was great when he learned that Tina Turner was born Annie Mae Bullock.

Watch out for too many "ins," "froms," "abouts," and "fors" when you're combining them with "which":

Bad Example: The food *for which* carnivorous plants yearn *for* is alive and kicking.

Good Example: The food *for which* carnivorous plants yearn is nothing I'd order for brunch.

Bad Example: Igloos are the only kind of shelter *in which* Carmenghia hesitates to live *in*.

Good Example: Igloos are the only kind of shelter *in which* Carmenghia hesitates to live.

Bad Example: The olives *from which* we get oil *from* don't contain pimientos.

Good Example: The olives *from which* we get oil don't contain pimientos.

Bad Example: Cecil's indiscretion, *about which* we are conferring *about* this morning, has really ticked off Candida.

Good Example: Cecil's indiscretion, *about which* we are conferring this morning, has really ticked off Candida (and who can blame her?).

BOTTOM LINE: Don't use words you don't need. Like rug fringes, they just attract dust.

"innovation," not "new innovation"

"refer to," not "refer back to"

"revert to," not "revert back to"

"proceed," not "proceed on" (same with "continue")

"reason," not "reason why" or "reason . . . because"

"fall off," not "fall off of"

"unique," not "more or most unique"

"take off," not "take off of"

don't say "one" unless you must

make sure you only use a single "in," "from," "about," and "for" with "which"

All R**i**g**h**t,

Al**rea**dy!

Alright" is not "already."
"Already" is one word. One *l*. Always.

"Alright" is one word, all right, but never mind what Webster's says—it's *unacceptable*. In the ninth grade, Henrietta Shilowitz handed in a paper including, "It was alright for Shakespeare's audience to eat fruit and throw the pits on the ground during the show," and Mrs. Krauss burst a blood vessel.

You want "all right." Two words. Two *l*s. Whether you're saying everything's hunky-dory or agreeing to drop off your mother's Enna Jetticks at the shoemaker's or agreeing with Cynthia that Raoul certainly *is* built like a brick wall, you want "all right." Read it with me:

All right!
All right!
   All right?
   All right!

BOTTOM LINE: *All right* is right. *Alright* is all wrong.

Afternoon at the Bureau of Proper Prepositions

"N ext."

Accused stepped forward. She slipped her preposition license under the protective glass that separated her from the clerk. In a strained voice, she explained, "I sent my ten dollars in for preposition renewal, and I got this in the mail a few days ago, and it's wrong, and I—"

"Gimme a minute to look at it, lady." The clerk eyed her with hostility. He looked at the card, opened a directory, scanned a few pages, closed the book, and pushed the license toward Accused. "You want window seventeen. Next!"

"But . . ." Accused began, but the man behind her elbowed her aside. Flustered, she looked around until she spotted window

17. With sinking spirits, Accused saw that the line extended the length of one long wall and then disappeared around a corner.

It was just too much. Disheartened, her last bit of energy and resolve panting on the floor, Accused began plodding toward the exit. She came within three or four feet of it when, lips aquiver, she stopped and simply stood there, tears spilling down her face.

"Miss, are you all right?" A security guard took her by the elbow. He was elderly, and Accused let him lead her to a water fountain off the main hall.

"Take a sip, miss. You'll feel better."

Schnuffling, Accused drank.

"There, see? Everything's gonna be all right."

"Thank you," Accused said, her voice trembling. "It's just so frustrating." They walked slowly back into the rotunda. "All these years I've been assigned 'Of.' Now, suddenly, they send me 'With.' Accused With? It's bad enough I have to go around defending myself all the time, but now this! What am I going to do?"

The guard put two fingers between his lips and gave a shrill whistle. Everyone in line ("on" line, if you're a New Yorker) turned.

"Listen up, people," the guard cried. "Help me to make things right for this young lady. She's Accused *OF.* Always has been." He began to applaud, slowly, chanting, "Accused *OF,* Accused *OF* . . ." One, then three, then dozens of citizens joined him, until Accused was awash in a heartening din.

The guard put his mouth to Accused's ear. "You see? You *are* Accused *OF.* Ain't no other preposition suit you so."

Cheered, standing just that much taller, Accused Of kissed the guard on the cheek, waved to the crowd, and with evanescent (fleeting!) determination and resolve, made her way to window 17.

For some reason, there is a current tendency to separate long-established couples and pair them with new partners who just don't jibe. Remember: You've got to leave with the date "what brung" you; put your hand back in the glove you took off; rinse out your own coffee cup.

For example:

➤ Vy was *accused of* an excessive interest in first aid. You cannot say, "Vy was *accused with* . . ."

You can only combine "accused" and "with" in the following way:

➤ Ty was accused with Vy of harboring hordes of bandages.

Or you can say:

➤ Also *accused in* the iodine scandal with Vy were Hy and his brother Sy.

Here are some other partnerships you must respect and not muck around with:

1. The Fucerils were *reluctant to* cross the Atlantic on a teeterboard. (*reluctant to,* not *reluctant in*)
2. "My son, Rutherford, *was graduated from* I.C.U.," crowed Mrs. Haze. Strictly speaking, you're supposed to say, "was/has been/will be graduated from," but you can get by with "graduated from," as in, "If you continue to skip Feelings 101, you will not *graduate from* this academy," the dean warned S. Kurt Chaser.

No one ever *graduated* Harvard, Kansas State, P.S. 208, Rivers Middle School, Churchill's Academy of Tai Kwon Do, or any other institution that issues a diploma.

You must graduate from
   graduate from
      graduate from
         graduate from
            GRADUATE FROM!

3. "When I *abide by* the rules, I'm very, very good. But when I disregard them, I'm horrid," said the brat with the curl. *Abide by* (follow), not simply abide. You can, however, say,

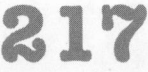

"Umberto could not abide (tolerate) seeing other people's bare feet."

4. Mr. Sandhaus held Mrs. Sandhaus *accountable for* (responsible for) keeping the hedgehogs fluffed. Mr. Sandhaus was *accountable to* (responsible to) Mrs. Sandhaus for every cotton ball he brought into the house.

5. The only time you *wait on* someone is when an eatery employs you to do so (or you're giving a party), as in, Princess Cabernet was forced to *wait on* tables when the queen got a bug up her you-know-what about the princess's spending habits.

    You do not *wait on* Uncle Hunt to let you know how many stiffs he's bringing for Halloween. You *wait for* Uncle Hunt to call, Aunt Dalmatia to cancel, and Cousin Durian to collapse.

6. More often than not, you also say: Sheldrake *prohibits* his team *from* celebrating in off-the-shoulder sheaths. It is, however, fine to say, The law *prohibits* a public display of merriment, unless the celebrants are accompanied by a passel of monkeys or a bevy of sailors.

When you're dealing with two of these hand-in-glove situations in one sentence, you cannot speed things up by leaving out one of the gloves. There are no shortcuts through these woods. You cannot say,

➤ Pixie Mint was sensitive and knowledgeable about splinters.
➤ Mr. Guttman is interested yet frightened of municipal statutes.

You must say,

➤ Pixie Mint was *sensitive to* and *knowledgeable about* splinters.
➤ Mr. Guttman is *interested in* yet *frightened of* municipal statutes.

BOTTOM LINE: After Doyle WAS GRADUATED FROM motel school, he booked himself into a string of motels across the country. He

was   INTERESTED IN

and   CURIOUS ABOUT

how these establishments were run, in general. Doyle, you see,

was   RELUCTANT TO

rush into business.

On his first stop out of town, he discovered that the basin in the bathroom was stopped up and the bedsheets wrinkled and discolored. The night clerk, however,

ACCUSED Doyle OF

being   RESPONSIBLE FOR

the mess himself. "Ya musta spit stuff down the sink, and how do I know ya dint walk all over the bed in ya shoes? The sheets was clean last month."

Doyle, however, was unwilling to

ABIDE BY

the night clerk's assessment. "Whoever runs this fleabag is

ACCOUNTABLE FOR

its upkeep," Doyle said hotly, "and if I have anything to say about it, he or she will be

PROHIBITED FROM

serving the public until these offenses are corrected."

The night clerk replied that the owner was not expected until the morning. "In that case, I shall

WAIT FOR

him or her here," said Doyle.

"Fine," said the clerk, "but don't keep calling me up every five minutes for dis and dat. It ain't in my job description to

WAIT ON

the guests."

"Fine!" replied Doyle, who sat up all night watching paid programming.

Why You Can't Say "These Premises Are Alarmed!"

F irst of all, what are you talking about? A frightened gas station? A panic-stricken jewelry store?

My guess is no. What you mean is

"Hear this, all you miscreants out there! Don't even *think* about breaking in here. We've got electrical alarms hidden all around to alert our crack security guard if you so much as put a toe where you don't belong. So beat it!"

Therefore, you want to say,

"These premises are *protected by* hair-trigger alarms (and a boa constrictor in a bad mood), so steer clear."

POINTED TIP: After you've written something, reread it and ask yourself: "What am I trying to say? Is that *actually* what I've said?"

BOTTOM LINE: "Blind Cleaning" doesn't mean "We Clean Blinds," does it, now?

Short Shrift,

If You Get

My Drift

TLC always felt it was her duty to be home when the kids got in from school. When the front door slammed, she called from the kitchen, "Is that you, RBI?"

"Yeah, Mom. I'm going over to ADW's house, okay?" His voice faded as he pounded up the stairs.

"Fine, but make sure you don't run around on the QT. You're not over that cold yet!"

She heard him thudding down the stairs. The front door opened and he hollered, "See you!" The front door banged.

TLC smiled. She rolled out another circle of pastry dough. Once again, the front door opened—and closed firmly, but not flamboyantly. "Hi, sweetie," called TLC. "I'm making chocolate snaps. Want to help?"

ERA skipped into the kitchen, toying with her braids.

"How was school?" asked TLC.

"PU," said ERA. "AC and DC, et al., said they'd try out for the boys' soccer team with me, but they chickened out at the last minute, and ETA was late for debating team practice, so I had to give the opening argument with no help."

"I'm sure you were A-one."

Just then, the phone rang. TLC wiped her hands and answered it. "Hi, dear, I'm so glad you called. Would you like partners for dinner, i.e., peas and carrots, rice and beans, etc.? Oh, MC, you always say that!" TLC laughed. "See you later, darling." She hung up. "Your father is the cat's PJs."

"Huh?"

"One in a million. A riot."

"Oh. That reminds me. Mr. Ampersand said Daddy should make an appointment to see him."

"Really? Why?"

ERA shrugged. "He said, 'in re that meeting' you all went to last week."

TLC tittered. "Your father was rather naughty. He made small jokes all the time, but then Mr. Ampersand went on and on ad nauseam about the need to raise money to attract a talented quarterback to Hollow Values HS football team. He could have made the same point concisely. I mean, it was an ad hoc committee meeting for that very purpose. And when your father moved to adjourn the meeting, Mr. Ampersand reacted as if Daddy were engaging in a nasty, ad hominem attack, rather than parliamentary procedure."

"Well," said ERA, popping a few chocolate chips into her mouth, "I'd better get going. I have lots of assignments to finish; e.g., an essay on anchorpeople and personal magnetism for my Media in Action class, and a chart on weight-loss products for Modern Nutrition." She grabbed a handful of chocolate chips.

"Dear, don't forget to RSVP to Mrs. Purview about Phelps's surprise party."

ERA nodded and skipped to her room.

Hurry up! Light a fire under it! Say what you want to licketysplit; this country didn't get where it is by lollygagging around!

Here are the most common shortcuts, which happen to be in Latin:

i.e.—that is, or that's to say (*id est*)

etc.—and so forth (*et cetera*, two words, yes, but for some reason they get squooshed together as "etc.")

e.g.—for example (*exempli gratia*)

et al.—and others (*et alia*)

ad hoc—for this particular purpose

ad hominem—personal, to the man

ad nauseam—to a stomach-turning degree

in re—concerning, or in regard to (from *res*, Latin for "thing")

If you're writing a story for *The Filthy Rag* and want to indicate that you'll fill in some missing information later on, use *TK*, which stands for "to come" or "to kum":

It was learned last night that the mayor's wife has been working as a stripper named Sultry Peppers at the Red Hot Club, which is owned by *TK*.

And, just so you know, these abbreviations mean the following, among other things:

TLC—tender loving care, The Learning Channel, Tom's Love Connection

RBI—runs batted in (baseball batters' stat), Reserve Bank of India, Remote Bus Isolator

ERA—earned run average (baseball pitchers' stat), Equal Rights Amendment, European Rum Association

ADW—assault with a deadly weapon (I've seen *Cops*), air defense weapon

QT—on the sly, secretly (from the first and last letters of "quiet")

PU—it stinks (I don't know where this comes from.)

A-1—the best (Some say this stands for "number *one*," as in "the best.")

AC—alternating current, area code, Air Canada.

DC—direct current, Detective Constable (Scotland Yard)

PJs—pajamas

MC—master of ceremonies, mission control

RSVP—please respond (from the French, "*Répondez, s'il vous plaît*"), the Research Society for Victorian Periodicals

HS—high school, head sling, Home Secretary (British)

BOTTOM LINE: If u cn rd ths, it dznt mttr.

Conclusion

And now, fond reader,
It's time to go.
I hope that you've had fun.
And if, what's more,
You've learned some things,
It looks like I done good.

If you've got other grammatical questions, I'd be happy to receive them, c/o:

Hyperion
114 Fifth Avenue
New York, NY 10011

Suggestion: Read

If you read good English, chances are you'll write and speak it, too (fingers crossed). So here—in no particular order—are some authors' works worth noting.

Robert Benchley. *The Benchley Roundup* by Nathaniel Benchley. University of Chicago Press, 1983.

J. D. Salinger. *Nine Stories*. Little, Brown & Company, 1991.

Willa Cather. *Great Short Works of Willa Cather*. HarperPerennial, 1993. (The last line of "Paul's Case" always knocks me out.)

Donald E. Westlake. *Why Me.* (No question mark. In the TOR Books, 1985, edition, page 35 is a gem.)

Mary Cantwell. *Manhattan, When I Was Young*. Houghton Mifflin Company, 1995. (And any of the columns she wrote for *The New York Times* during the 1980s.)

Philip Roth. *Goodbye, Columbus* (and five terrific stories). The Modern Library, 1995.

Rumer Godden. *Kingfishers Catch Fire*. Milkweed Editions, 1994. (I'd read a menu, if she wrote it.)

Mary Renault. *Fire from Heaven*. Vintage Books, 1977. (Meet Alexander the Great and his mom and dad.)

John le Carré. *A Perfect Spy*. Alfred A. Knopf, 1986.

Thomas Harris. *The Silence of the Lambs*. St. Martin's Paperbacks, 1989. (Even if you've seen the film, keep a lot of lights on.)

Edith Wharton. *The House of Mirth*. Vintage Books, 1990.

Mark Twain. *Penguin Classics: Tales, Speeches, Essays & Sketches*.

1994. (His saber work in "Fenimore Cooper's Literary Offenses" is particularly breathtaking.)

Flannery O'Connor. *The Complete Stories.* Farrar, Straus & Giroux, 1971. (Not when you're depressed.)

Herman Melville. "Bartleby." Penguin, 1995. (A short story; forget the whale.)

Shirley Jackson. *We Have Always Lived in the Castle.* Viking Penguin, 1984. (Just as haunting as *The Haunting of Hill House.*)

Voltaire. *Candide.* Signet Classic, 1961. (In English, of course.)

Note: If you detect a grammatical error in any of the above—and you will—give yourself a high five. No one's grammatically perfect all the time (except, perhaps, Roth, Salinger, Cantwell, and a couple of the others). In fact, Godden, Renault, and other British authors I've read often inexplicably link two independent sentences with a comma, as in: "He wore a yellow ribbon, there was no time to get the tiara." And Ms. Renault used "further" for "farther." Like a lot of others, she also used "which" for "that." Go figure.

Index

Ellie Grossman is a freelance writer who wrote a freewheeling lifestyle column that was syndicated throughout North America by Newspaper Enterprise Association for ten years.

She's also the author of a published novel, which she regrets: "My rent went up and I wrote it in three months. If I'd realized it was going to be reviewed as a 'first novel,' I'd have used a pseudonym."

She does not regret writing her book *Lawyers from Hell,* or writing for the New York *Daily News, Ladies' Home Journal, Cosmopolitan,* and other publications; or that the BBC World Service broadcast her short story "Golden Days" in English and Chinese; or that, a few years ago, Malice Domestic nominated her short story "Amanda" as best short story (it appeared in *Alfred Hitchcock Mystery Magazine*); or that a few months ago *Newsweek* published her "My Turn."

She belongs to The Authors Guild and the American Society of Journalists and Authors.

She is also a native New Yorker who says "on" line.